At the
End of the
Day

Text copyright © David Winter 2013
The author asserts the moral right
to be identified as the author of this work

Published by
The Bible Reading Fellowship
15 The Chambers, Vineyard
Abingdon OX14 3FE
United Kingdom
Tel: +44 (0)1865 319700
Email: enquiries@brf.org.uk
Website: www.brf.org.uk
BRF is a Registered Charity

ISBN 978 0 85746 057 8

First published 2013
Reprinted 2014
10 9 8 7 6 5 4 3 2 1

Acknowledgments
Unless otherwise stated, scripture quotations are taken from the New Revised Standard
Version of the Bible, Anglicised edition, copyright © 1989, 1995 by the Division of Christian
Education of the National Council of the Churches of Christ in the United States of America,
and are used by permission. All rights reserved.

Extracts from the Authorised Version of the Bible (The King James Bible), the rights in which
are vested in the Crown, are reproduced by permission of the Crown's Patentee, Cambridge
University Press.

Cover photo: Comstock

A catalogue record for this book is available from the British Library

Printed and bound by CPI Group (UK) Ltd, Croydon CR0 4YY

At the
End of the
Day

Enjoying life
in the departure lounge

David
Winter

Contents

Introduction

I can name, almost to the day, the moment when I reluctantly accepted that I was old—not 'senior' or 'mature', not elderly or getting on a bit, but old. It was in April 2012 and I was walking along the Broadway in my home town, Thatcham, in Berkshire. I glanced at a shop window and saw the reflection of an old man walking. As I put my head down into the wind (it was a very cold day), I realised with a shock that it was me.

So, I'm 'old'. It's not a term we like to apply to ourselves or even to others, although I shall unashamedly and proudly use it throughout this book. 'Old' was once a compliment and to be old an honoured achievement—indeed, the older the better. In any case, facts are facts. I have joined a large and growing segment of people in British society who (whatever euphemism we employ to disguise the fact) are indisputably old. No less than 1.4 million people in the UK are aged 85 or over, and that figure is set to rise year on year. Average life expectancy for men is now 78.2 years and for women 82.3, with the gap narrowing each year. Practically, it means that a man or woman who reaches 70 in reasonably good health will probably join the ranks of the octogenarians—and beyond. It is estimated that by 2020 there will be at least 20,000 centenarians in Britain. Buckingham Palace will be kept busy with all those cards of congratulation!

I remember, as a child, being taken by my parents to visit an elderly great-aunt who had reached her 90th birthday. My brothers and I were ushered into her presence to see this astonishing sight. What we actually gazed at was a crumpled figure, eyes weak and watering, skin wrinkled and sallow, who couldn't hear what we said or see clearly enough to know who we were. More than anything else, it left us quite sure that whatever else happened to us, we didn't want to live to 90.

Yet now, in my usual seat in church, I have two 90-year-old ladies sitting behind me. They are lively and friendly, fully involved in all that goes on, not only in church but in the town and the world beyond. The contrast is astonishing—and they are not the only people of that age in the congregation. In my last parish there was a 90-year-old woman who regularly cycled to church (until she fell off and my wife persuaded her to accept a lift). Old age is no longer the prerogative of the favoured few and is not necessarily marked by physical or mental decay.

So, sooner or later, if we are 'spared', as my grandmother used to put it, we shall grow old. All the modern mantras about 70 being the 'new 60', all the oils and pills and Botox and all the amazing devices of the National Health Service cannot alter the date on my birth certificate. As my excellent GP put it as he checked my latest blood test, 'David, you may not look 82, but your kidneys are.' Oh, and not only my kidneys! The body I have lived in for four-score years frequently reminds me, rather like the ominous sounds from the engine or transmission of an old car, that the miles on the clock tell their story. So do the eyes and the ears and the lungs. If the bus beats me to the stop, I let it go. I've given up doing a geriatric sprint and spending the rest of the journey trying to get my breath back. After all, there'll be another one in 30 minutes, and what's that in the eyes of eternity?

This is not the attitude that has shaped most of my life. Time has been my dictator: the diary, the calendar, the deadlines and the appointments. I remember now, with the fond acceptance of old age, that I am the rector who raged if the service started 30 seconds late, whose homily had to end as the church clock struck ten, whose proudest achievement in broadcasting was the boast that however bad the programme he produced, at least it started and ended on time.

Then and now

But now I am old. That was then, and this is now. Those readers of roughly my own age will know what I'm talking about in this book and will perhaps enjoy the telling, but I hope that those who are not quite there might value a positive peep into what lies ahead. In the wonderful television series *Outnumbered*, the mouthy little girl asked her grandpa, 'What's it like being old?' He paused and then replied, 'Well, it beats being dead.' Actually, I'm not sure it does, as we shall see, but like most people I'm not in a hurry to find out. Until that day, I simply go on experiencing yet another part of life's unstoppable roundabout—infancy, childhood, adolescence, young adulthood, 'prime', middle age, seniority and then, if one is still on the wooden horse, old age. Each has its joys; each has its anxieties and stresses; each moves seamlessly into the next. Believe it or not, being old can be fun.

That last statement may seem incredible. We don't associate 'fun' with slowing down, with wonky knees and hips, forgetfulness, bladder problems, cataracts, hearing aids and incontinence pads, though the popular TV series *Getting On* suggests that they can provide a rich source of comedy. For my generation, those very things, so daunting when listed, can also be the raw material of endless banter and countless anecdotes, to be told conspiratorially only among those for whom they are (or might soon be) the stuff of life. I honestly think I've laughed more since I was 80—often with my fellow octogenarians—than I did during my 20 years at the BBC.

Fair enough, you may think, but why would anyone who's not there yet want to know about it? Why, when life is good and its powers are at their zenith, should I want to think about anything as depressing as getting old?

In fact, until relatively modern times, old age was not regarded as depressing, but as a rich privilege, even a sign of divine blessing. It had its drawbacks but age was credited with wisdom born of experience, with patience and a kind of dignity. The really old were treated with something approaching awe.

Being old in the modern world

In contrast, the elderly in the modern Western world are regarded (even by themselves, sometimes) largely as problems, actual or potential. Apparently, there are simply too many of us. Commentators go on about the 'geriatric explosion' as though somewhere a horde of crazed octogenarians are about to launch a bomb into our well-ordered society. Why should anyone want to explore being old when it involves such public disapproval?

People are living longer and that inevitably means there will be increased demands on the health service, sheltered housing and care homes. Pension schemes are stretched by the obstinate refusal of old people to die and so help to keep their funds in balance. No one has yet proposed a cull of all those over a certain age (although the film Logan's Run, about 30 years ago, was based on precisely that premise). All the same, it's sometimes difficult for the elderly not to feel that they are, if not an intolerable burden, at least a bit of a nuisance and a serious drain on society's resources.

This is not simply a matter of finance, needless to say. Families face the problem of an elderly grandparent who is no longer capable of caring for herself. Hospitals face the problem of 'bed-blocking' by elderly patients who can't be sent home but don't really need to be in hospital. If all of that is what being old entails, we may ask, why concern ourselves with it before we get there? 'Sufficient unto the day...' and all that.

Fortified by pills from the doctor and an occasional hospital visit for running repairs, we who are indisputably old may not feel that we shall ever be a burden (or a 'bed-blocker'), though one never knows, of course. Indeed, the great majority of old people do not end up in nursing homes and many of us would say that life is as fulfilling now as it was 30 years ago, while being profoundly different. The premise of this book, put simply, is that if you find you are still here, it's best to make the most of it—and that 'the most of it' is not as awful as anticipation might suggest. I suppose a third premise must be confessed. I think that faith (to be defined later) is very often the key to a fulfilling old age.

Geraphobia

Despite that, most of us, at some time in our lives, experience 'gerophobia', the fear of being old. Its most obvious symptoms are cosmetic: for men, Viagra, the 'cures' for baldness and shampoos to darken the hair; for women—well, where do we start? There is a whole industry geared to persuading women that they can delay or even permanently repel the tide of the years or, at any rate, their outward symptoms. Advertisements promise everything from the eradication of wrinkles to a completely 'new' face, firm and youthful. Men as well as women are persuaded to embark on costly and risky surgery to correct the visible evidence of the passing years. 'For 20 grand,' someone said to me recently, 'you can look 20 years younger', but there is no sum of money that can actually reverse the calendar. We are what we are.

In the same hopeless cause, older men and women are tempted to ape the styles, customs and vocabulary of the young. Perhaps if the skirt is short enough, the jeans tight enough, the tattoos vivid enough, we shall be accepted as members of the younger set. If we can Tweet and do Facebook, if we can name a favourite band (preferably a rather rude one), if we can use the strange language of the networking age with its LOLs and BTWs, we might be accepted as full members of contemporary society rather than washed-out spectators on its shore. Just for the record, I've tried most of them and they don't really work.

In parallel, we have a general reluctance to use the vocabulary of age about ourselves or those whose approval we cherish. We become 'senior citizens', the people of the 'third age', 'retired' but definitely not out. That's fair enough, I suppose, but it does imply that actually to be 'old' is an unmentionable fate.

All of this contributes to our fear of age. This is not the same thing as the fear of dying (though they may sometimes be connected). It is more to do with our sense of self-worth, the product of a culture that has forgotten how to respect old age and how to approach it positively. It is fear of vulnerability, of helplessness, of diminution and loss of respect and status. Yet at 82 I am still the same person as

I was at 22, 42 and 62. The body creaks, the memory is sometimes a bit sluggish (like an overworked computer), but the character they serve is still here, distinct and individual, replete with the memories of all those years but living now.

Of course, what we know about being old is based either on our own experience of it (if we've reached that stage in life) or what we have learnt from the experiences of others. One thing is certain, though: what we are in old age is shaped, to a greater or lesser extent, by what we have been through all the earlier episodes of life.

The amazing television documentary most recently entitled *56 Up* has followed the lives of a carefully selected group of children from the time they were seven in 1963. In 2012 they had reached 56, hence the title. Every seven years it has tracked them down and recorded their experiences, feelings, joys and tragedies. It has been a powerful reminder that, like it or not, we are shaped by our 'lived history'. The adolescent is shaped by his or her childhood, the adult by adolescent experience, the middle-aged by their experience of adulthood. Some have encountered major changes in life, even profound transformations of personality. Yet it is still fundamentally true, as Tennyson puts it in the mouth of Ulysses, that 'I am a part of all that I have been' (*Poems*, 1842). At 80 I don't become someone else.

Life experience

That's why it seemed right to start this book with a quick reprise of my own life experience, because clearly that has shaped not only who I have been but who I am now. It also colours my perception of old age (and hence these pages). The reader is surely entitled to know what I bring into the final baggage hall of life, what influences have led to my life choices and shape my view of the present (and the future).

The 'experience of others' is, in a way, trickier. Many—probably most—great writers have offered insights into what old age is like or would be like. They will surface in this book from time to time, but I shall take as my first spreadsheet, as it were, the story of age as recounted in the books of the Bible. After all, there is no more extensive record of human experience anywhere in literature than that offered by the often anonymous writers of the Hebrew and Christian scriptures. They cover, in story, poetry and chronicle, over three millennia of human history, from the nomadic days of the early patriarchs through to the subtle and sophisticated influences of classic Greco-Roman culture. I'm not turning to them, in this instance, to expound divine law or promote Christian doctrine, but as memorable and illuminating stories from the distant past of our race, which offer fascinating insights into what it has always meant to people to be old.

We shall find that, in ancient times, old age was treated with deference. No one seems to have noted that old people can be awkward, forgetful, untidy and even occasionally smelly. It is a sanitised picture—or perhaps a spiritualised one, because the elderly were seen as receptacles of rich blessing. Nevertheless, the ancient world, the world of the patriarchs, prophets and evangelists, was also brutally frank about two things. Firstly, old age brings responsibility. Secondly, it inevitably ends in physical decline and death. Those are insights that today's world cannot afford to ignore, however much it may wish to.

To that record we shall need to add the experience of today, the changed perceptions and circumstances brought about by where we are and the sort of society we live in now.

But those insights and stored wisdom are for later. For now, let me offer a brief sketch of the circumstances, ideas and people who have shaped my own life. After all, it's the only one I know 'from the inside'.

1

Meet the old man

I was born in 1929, the year of the Wall Street Crash, probably the worst financial catastrophe of the 20th century. I spent my early childhood in Wood Green, a nondescript suburb of north London, now part of the London Borough of Haringey. I was the middle one of three sons. My father was a clerk in the Ministry of Labour, as it was then called. My mother, in the manner of the time, ran the home.

In 1939 I was evacuated, along with the rest of the school (including my five-year-old brother), to a village in Essex, but, when an invasion from the Continent seemed likely, our parents wisely decided that a location right in the path of the oncoming German army seemed a touch impractical and arranged for us to go and live with my grandparents in rural central Wales.

When I say 'rural', I mean it: the house was two up, two down, with no piped water, no flushing toilets, no electricity or telephones. Yet those few years were wonderfully rewarding to me. I came to appreciate the beauty of our surroundings, the richness of the simple life, the fun of the outdoors and the wonderful sense of a small but close-knit community of people who really cared for each other. As a bonus, I learnt to speak Welsh—my grandmother's native tongue and the language of the village school, even for learning sums. I went on to the grammar school in the nearest town, Machynlleth, coming back to London only when my parents decided that the air raids were a thing of the past. In fact, I came home to Wood Green to be greeted by Hitler's 'secret weapons', his last desperate throw of the dice—the V1 and V2 rockets.

National Service followed (as an RAF nursing assistant) and, after that, university, at King's College, London, where I read English. That was hardly onerous for a young man who simply loved words. An important event during my student days was an experience of Christian conversion, which has remained with me all my life and has largely shaped it from then on.

Before I reached the end of the course at King's, my father died—the long-term victim of gassing 35 years earlier during World War I. After university (and the Post-Graduate Education Certificate) I taught for five years, in Hertfordshire and then back in London, while harbouring desperate hopes of a career one day in journalism.

I did quite a lot of freelance writing, and then, like a favour from the Good Fairy, a phone call offered me the post of editor of Britain's first full-colour glossy Christian magazine, *Crusade*. (You wouldn't call it that now!) Within a year I was married to Christine, a young community nurse. I had eleven years working at *Crusade*, until eventually another late-flowering ambition was realised and a phone call recruited me as a producer in the religious broadcasting department of BBC Radio. The department had launched a weekly religious news magazine programme, *Sunday*, and journalistic help was welcome.

I stayed at the BBC for 20 years, as producer, editor, television producer and finally Head of Religious Broadcasting. It was sometimes hectic, sometimes fraught and generally satisfying, in a high-tension kind of way. Sadly, work meant that I saw a great deal less of our family (two sons and a daughter) than I would have liked, but we had acquired a holiday cottage in Wales (where else?) and we all spent time there whenever gaps appeared in the diary.

From my student days and the dawn of a committed Christian faith, I had admitted the possibility that ordination might lie ahead for me at some point, but by now I was in my 50s. Surely I'd missed that particular bus? It was our area bishop, Bill Westwood, who persuaded me that with God it is never 'too late'. I went to a selection conference, was recommended for training and, in 1985, enrolled in the part-time ordination course at Oak Hill Theological College, London. The course completed, and with Christine's enthusiastic agreement, I took (slightly) early retirement from the BBC and we moved to Oxfordshire to start yet another career—this time, together (Christine was a licensed lay minister).

My eleven years as a parish priest were, without a shadow of a doubt, the happiest and most fulfilling of my life. The very things that, for years, had made me question my aptitude for priesthood turned out to be those that I found most rewarding—being with people at crucial moments in their lives, helping men and women to find faith, praying with the sick and ministering to the dying. In an odd kind of way, I feel that in my 60s I finally grew up.

That brings the story of my life to the year 2000, when I retired from licensed ministry. I've continued to take services, lead retreats, baptise, marry and conduct funerals: until he or she can't stand up any longer, a priest will always have such opportunities, and, as a late starter, I cherish them. Christine died in 2001, before we could enjoy the full fruits of retirement together. By then we had two lovely grandchildren.

What do I do now? I suppose one answer is, I'm simply here, with memories and recollected joys, living (so far) in my own little house, not far from my daughter and her family. She is rector of six nearby parishes, not having prevaricated as long as her father about responding to the call. I write rather a lot, do a little broadcasting from time to time, but most of all enjoy some of the simplicity I found long ago in rural Wales.

This, of course, is only the story of events. Life is much more than that, and a true picture of a whole personality can't be summarised in a list of schools, qualifications, jobs, family, health and so on. My personal picture must include a love of words (poetry, drama, novels, biography), the lifeblood of friendship, love and family, and the rich blessing of faith. I've always been a bit impatient and am now rapidly becoming a Grumpy Old Man. I like sport—cricket and football to watch, but once upon a time I played hockey quite seriously. My musical tastes are broad and probably sentimental, if I'm honest—grand opera, Mendelssohn and Rachmaninov, the Beach Boys, Bee Gees and Westlife. I also like television comedy and Alan Ayckbourn plays at the theatre.

Nothing in the week, in my dotage, surpasses the Sunday morning Eucharist, however. In a new way, heaven opens and I feel absolutely at home.

That's more or less where I am as I write this book. I appreciate that I have had many opportunities in life that have been denied to others. Some of those reading my story will feel that it's the record of someone determined to have a public role, for all my talk of simplicity. I think I might agree. I have made many blunders and let many people down. But it is me, and that is the 'me' who is now looking at what it means for 'me'—and my readers—to be old.

Alongside personal experience, the basic resource of this book, as I have said, is the Bible. That long record of human experience offers no single pattern or programme for old age. The people in it lived their lives as we live ours. You are you, as I am me, and they are characters from a vast archive, distant in time but profoundly human. We can recognise the hallmarks. Our shared humanity means that, at some point, all experiences of life, including those of being old, will reflect common elements—bits and pieces of the private picture that are, in fact, public possessions.

In any case, the time has come to put my own story in a drawer and bring out instead the wisdom of the ancients and the experience of the longer vision. I start with the stories of old people that we find in the Bible, both the Old Testament and the New, and ask what they reveal about the way being old was understood in those far-off times and also whether they offer a particular—or indeed universal—insight into what it means to be old.

2

The pitcher is broken at the fountain

Remember your creator in the days of your youth, before the days of trouble come, and the years draw near when you will say, 'I have no pleasure in them'; before the sun and the light and the moon and the stars are darkened and the clouds return with the rain; in the day when the guards of the house tremble, and the strong men are bent, and the women who grind cease working because they are few, and those who look through the windows see dimly; when the doors on the street are shut, and the sound of the grinding is low, and one rises up at the sound of a bird, and all the daughters of song are brought low; when one is afraid of heights, and terrors are in the road; the almond tree blossoms, the grasshopper drags itself along and desire fails; because all must go to their eternal home, and the mourners will go about the streets; before the silver cord is snapped, and the golden bowl is broken, and the pitcher is broken at the fountain, and the wheel broken at the cistern, and the dust returns to the earth as it was, and the breath returns to God who gave it.

ECCLESIASTES 12:1–7

Perhaps because I love poetry or possibly because, throughout life, I've liked to leave the nicest bits till last (eat the crust, then the jam), I've chosen to turn first not to the stories of the long-lived patriarchs and the awestruck reverence with which the ancient world viewed old age, but instead to a beautiful, wistful but ultimately rather gloomy picture of what it means to be old. It's found towards the end of the book of Ecclesiastes (the title means 'Preacher'). The writer depicts human life as 'vanity' and human effort as pointless striving against the inevitable. The pleasure that God does give lies in our toil, in our glimpses of ultimate truth and in obedience to the voice of his wisdom.

Then, right at the end of his book, the Preacher addresses his younger readers, urging them to find that divine wisdom before it is too late, because lying ahead of them is the dreadful spectre of decline, decay and death. It's a miserable theme but the language is memorable and disturbingly perceptive. We sense that the writer knows what he's talking about from personal experience.

In a series of metaphors he describes the effects of ageing, so cleverly that a casual reader might miss some of the points altogether. Hebrew scholars have disputed the meaning of some of his metaphorical images but the overall theme is clear enough. The catalogue of decline is precise and horribly familiar to most of us who are old.

First of all we have the bald statement that the time will come when we can't see any pleasure to be gained from the passing days. The Preacher then describes a growing difficulty in distinguishing objects, even those as obvious as moon, stars and sun. Then there are the trembling limbs ('the guards of the house'), back trouble ('the strong men are bent') and the loss of teeth ('the women who grind... are few'). The voice becomes squeaky like a bird's and hearing declines so that it's as if the sounds on the street are being heard through a closed door. The elderly become unsteady on their feet and tend to fall over, so going outdoors becomes hazardous. The hair (if we've got any) goes white like an almond tree in blossom. 'The grasshopper drags it-self along'—a suitably obscure metaphor that Jewish rabbis have traditionally applied to sexual impotence, likening the droopy grasshopper to a by-now-useless male organ.

The picture of decline ends, of course, in the only way possible—death. All must go to their eternal home and the mourners must go about the streets. The images of brokenness multiply. Precious things, sources of life and beauty—golden bowls, pitchers, silver cords, cistern wheels—are all broken and useless. Finally the body itself joins them. Made of dust, it returns to the dust, and the breath that God gave it returns to its source. 'Vanity of vanities, says the Teacher; all is vanity' (v. 8).

It's an uncompromising end to an uncompromising book. In the long experience of life and death that the Bible chronicles, this is its most pessimistic moment—though even here there constantly lurks the presence and voice of God, the giver (and taker) of life. It seemed to me a suitably robust and painfully honest start to our investigation into the way the Hebrew and Christian scriptures deal with these issues. No one can accuse the old Preacher of offering 'pie in the sky when you die'. For him, there isn't much pie down here to start with.

We must set it in context, of course. At this stage in the development of the Jewish faith, there was little notion of life beyond death. The dead simply went to Sheol, the 'pit'. No one seemed to know exactly what that meant, but one psalmist took the view that its residents were in effect non-persons: 'I am counted among those who go down to the Pit; I am like those who have no help, like those forsaken among the dead, like the slain that lie in the grave, like those whom you remember no more, for they are cut off from your hand' (Psalm 88:4–5).

There are hints of something more hopeful, including the frequent Old Testament description of so-and-so 'going to their fathers', but no coherent belief in an afterlife. That belief does not emerge until the writings of the great Hebrew prophets, notably Daniel, Ezekiel and Isaiah, several centuries later. By the time of Jesus, resurrection (at the 'last day') was the received faith of most Jews, the Sadducees being the notable exceptions. Belief in resurrection was not articulated in the first five books of the Bible (the Pentateuch), which was why the Sadducees rejected it.

That is the biblical context. The historical context is of a society where remedies that today's advanced world takes for granted were unknown— opticians, dentists, physiotherapy, hearing aids and drugs to combat or hold back conditions like dementia or palsy. The old were sheltered in the bosom of the extended family, fed, cared for and respected but not expected to do much at all (beyond giving the next generation the finest jewels of their hard-earned wisdom, of course). That was more or less the lot of the elderly until modern times, and there are many pictures of it in characters in novels and plays. Perhaps the best-known is Shakespeare's 'Seven ages of man' speech in *As You Like It*, which lists the various stages of life and describes the final one—that of second childhood—as being 'sans teeth, sans eyes, sans taste, sans everything'.

This does not mean that the ancient poem in Ecclesiastes is irrelevant to readers today. The truth is that decline—physical and mental—is built into our DNA. Our world may be better at warding off its symptoms but they are still ultimately irresistible. It is sheer delusion to imagine that advancing years do not take their toll of energy, mental agility and bodily strength. A contented old age is not achieved by pretending that things are not as they are or will not follow their natural course. There are, as we shall see, compensations—very considerable ones—to being old, but they are balanced with penalties, as our experience from childhood to old age tells us that each stage of life will bring.

Eventually, as Ecclesiastes so eloquently puts it, the 'silver cord' is broken. The aged body with all its infirmities goes to its 'eternal home' and the mourners gather in the street. The body gives back its precious handful of dust to the earth and the lungs breathe their last: the 'spirit' returns to its Giver. There is a kind of completeness here, but, taken at face value, nothing to make being old seem anything but a preparation for being dead.

The difference between this poem in Ecclesiastes and a contemporary one in Sumerian culture is the mysterious and constant presence of God through the whole process. The One who first gave the gift of life seems to brood over its existence. The young man to whom the poem is addressed must 'remember his Creator' and it is the Creator who gathers up the dust and the spirit at the end of the earthly journey. Perhaps, at that stage in history, no one really knew what he was planning to do with them, but God does not die and his purposes are not limited by the span of a human life. I think even the first readers of this poem sensed that there was more to the story than decline, decay and death.

3

Back to Methuselah, or 'Do numbers matter?'

When Enoch had lived for sixty-five years, he became the father of Methuselah. Enoch walked with God after the birth of Methuselah for three hundred years, and had other sons and daughters. Thus all the days of Enoch were three hundred and sixty-five years. Enoch walked with God; then he was no more, because God took him. When Methuselah had lived for one hundred and eighty-seven years, he became the father of Lamech. Methuselah lived after the birth of Lamech for seven hundred and eighty-two years, and had other sons and daughters. Thus all the days of Methuselah were nine hundred and sixty-nine years; and he died.

GENESIS 5:21–27

Human beings have always had a strange fascination with 'numerical age'. You can see it in the words above, probably first penned well over 3000 years ago, but the most casual glance at your newspaper will reveal that the fascination still endures. 'John Thomas, 46, was found guilty yesterday of driving while uninsured... A 77-year-old pedestrian was knocked down in Bromley High Street by a car driven by a 19-year-old student... Well-known TV personality Jonathan Grubb died yesterday. He was 65.' Sometimes the age does have a relevance; often it does not. It's simply there because we like to know it.

It's not only in the press, in any case. 'How old is he?' is one of the first questions we ask about someone; and while there are times when we wish people didn't know our age, at other times we are happy to see it advertised. Scrawled messages at roundabouts tell the world that 'Liz is 40!'

Then there are the people, mostly of about my age, who will ask you to guess how old they are. This is a tricky one. You don't want to hurt their feelings by guessing that they are older than they actually are, especially as the whole point of their request is to surprise you with how young they look. My usual ploy is to estimate their actual age (often quite difficult) and then subtract anything up to ten years. Done with conviction, this can make somebody's day. 'Well, actually,' they say triumphantly, 'I'm 92!' The correct response to that is a look of utter astonishment and even some such phrase as 'Are you really?'

When I was in hospital for heart surgery a few years ago, the surgeon (Professor of Cardiac Surgery at Oxford University, no less) arrived at my bedside with his troupe of adoring students. Having explained to them, in gruesome detail, my original plight and the astonishing bodily plumbing he had done to correct it, he had one final question for them. 'How old do you think this gentleman is?' At this I was all ears. They guessed various figures, all reassuringly below my actual age. They left me in a glow of satisfaction, until I realised that what I had just experienced was a brilliantly executed seminar in bedside manners.

Anyway, there's no doubt that age, counted in numbers, fascinates us, as it clearly did the chronicler in these early chapters of Genesis. The playwright Bernard Shaw, over a century ago, wrote a play called *Back to Methuselah*. Its central argument was that human progress is held back because we don't live long enough. By the time we've acquired a bit of genuine wisdom, we die. So his answer was to go 'back to Methuselah', to enable the old to live long enough to impart the wisdom that can only be accumulated by experience. I read the play as a student, when I was about 20, and remember thinking that although it was an interesting idea, it didn't seem obvious that wisdom automatically grows with age.

In the century since Shaw's play was written, the lifespan of the average resident of the developed nations has increased by about 15 per cent, but it is not immediately evident that our society is any wiser. Cleverer, yes; technically more advanced and fiendishly good at instant communication, marketing and guided missiles—but wiser? The case has yet to be proved.

On the other hand, think what the world would have lost if certain people had died earlier. Michelangelo was appointed architect of St Peter's Rome at 79 and designed his last church when he was 88. Nelson Mandela became President of the newly democratic South Africa at the age of 75. Claude Monet completed his famous 'Water Lily' series of paintings at 85 and Picasso was still painting at 91.

So perhaps Bernard Shaw has a case. It's worth noting that none of those notable elderly people (to whom we could have added the saintly Mother Teresa, still leading her work among the poor in Calcutta at the age of 86) was a scientist or technician. Their skills and gifts were artistic, social or spiritual, well honed in the long years of application and experience, themselves often painful and costly. Nevertheless, the human race would have lost much of enormous value had they all died in their 60s.

This brings us, in a way, back to Methuselah. What on

earth do these ancient texts from Genesis say to us about being old? Obviously, they are not to be taken factually. This is prehistory, literally antediluvian. These early chapters of Genesis are picking up strands from the creation narratives and running with them. Adam and Eve and their children had children, they say. We have had the line of the murderer, Cain; now we have the line of Seth. Genealogies in the Bible are seldom even intended to be straight history. They are concerned with status, dignity, connection. Common to these primitive genealogies is longevity: in fact, everyone (except poor Abel, murdered by his brother Cain) lived so long that generations overtook each other. Adam was still alive in the days of Lamech, nine generations later. Their ages were reckoned not in years but centuries, with the legendary Methuselah clocking up the absolute record, 969.

Some nameless evil (at least, its identity is a mystery to biblical scholars) corrupted the human race, and God then decreed that 'their days shall be one hundred and twenty years' (Genesis 6:3). That's about an 89 per cent reduction from Methuselah's age! Gradually the Bible's story works towards the psalmist's 'three score years and ten' (Psalm 90:10, KJV), although, as we shall see, great heroes were invariably reported to have lived to a much greater age.

That, surely, is the point that the chronicler (or chroniclers, for this text had many editors over the centuries) is trying to make. It's not, as they see it, that 'the good die young', but that the good live and live and live. Long life was seen as a direct reward from God (see, for instance, Deuteronomy 6:2; Psalm 91:16; Proverbs 3:16) and the seal on a godly life was to 'go to your fathers' at the end of a fruitful and lengthy old age. The fact that some did, in fact, die young is generally glossed over in the Hebrew scriptures, unless the death was in combat. Old age was therefore associated with wisdom, righteousness and the blessing of God. It was to be respected. Remember what happened to the youngsters who teased the prophet Elisha about his bald head (2 Kings 2:23–25)!

There is, of course, a deeper truth behind this apparent obsession with longevity. Right at the beginning of the Genesis creation story, we have that most vivid picture of God scooping a handful of dust from the ground to shape the first human and then, crucially, breathing into his nostrils 'the breath of life' (Genesis 2:7). Thus life is to be treated with reverence and awe, because it is the gift of God.

If that is what life truly is, then the biblical authors argued that the more you have of it, the more you have received of a divine gift. Right at the start of things, as it were, the principle is established that life is precious because God gives it. He alone is the 'life-giver'. Therefore (for instance) to take the life of another is the most dreadful of sins, because it offends against the fundamental truth that humans are made in the image of God and their lives are his gift. The words are stark and awesome: 'Whoever sheds the blood of a human, by a human shall that person's blood be shed; for in his own image God made humankind' (Genesis 9:6).

Seeing life—long or short—as gift is not simply an abstract theological principle. It affects the way we live. Indeed, it shapes practice and policy. If the life I am living now is the gift of God, then it follows that it should be gratefully received. There will be times when life seems a burden and times when we may feel that we have had enough of it, but, if it is the gift of our Creator, then even at those moments we are alive with the life of God. It is still a precious gift.

We can see this principle in the way human beings respect

the lives of others. Human society at its best treats life as precious: indeed, people will even risk their own lives to save someone else's. We value the work of doctors and nurses, paramedics and lifeboat crews. We honour those who jump into the sea to rescue a drowning child without thought for their own safety. We regard loss of life as the most grievous of all events, but sometimes it is harder to see the other side of that truth: if all human life is so precious, then the particular life of each one of us is also precious.

Life is precious for the child, full of potential, bursting with energy and curiosity. It is precious for the adolescent, tasting the privileges and perils of new experiences, relationships and responsibilities. It is precious for the young parent, for the middle-aged and for the mature. Sometimes, however (and I'm thinking of a recent conversation with a lady of my own age), it is harder for the elderly to see that the days of twilight, when health and strength begin to decline and memory to fail, are equally part of that precious gift of life. That is what makes people dread growing old, and that is what leads some old people to feel as if their lives have become pointless, with days and weeks and months to be endured rather than enjoyed. These are issues to which we shall return.

How did Methuselah feel at, say, 963? It's a meaningless question. If indeed he did live to a tremendous old age, was he still full of vigour or did he, like the rest of us, begin to suffer physical and mental slowdown—the mists of dementia, the loss of mobility, the inevitable aches and pains that accompany the ageing process? If it's bad at 82, what would it be like at 963?

As soon as we move out of the antediluvian period and into something we can at least recognise as history, biblical ages become recognisably 'normal'. The psalmist, 3000 years ago, summarised the human lifespan thus: 'The days of our life are seventy years, or perhaps eighty, if we are strong; even then their span is only toil and trouble; they are soon gone, and we fly away' (90:10). In fact, anthropologists reckon that the lifespan of the average male at that time fell far short of 70, as it has done throughout history until the era of modern medicine and health care in Western societies. Nevertheless, those whom the psalmist calls 'strong' were objects of profound respect. Their lives may have been full of 'toil and trouble', but the gift of life was still theirs. In a culture where there was no clear notion of any life beyond the grave, that was cause for celebration.

4

Some ancient case studies

Abraham and Sarah

Well before the days of the psalmists, we have the stories of Abraham and Sarah, then Moses. All three cast interesting light on the way old age was regarded at the time. They also provide an insight into the way women (in a fiercely patriarchal society) saw their own role as they reached old age.

Let's take first the story of Abraham and his wife Sarah. Having migrated from Ur of the Chaldees to Canaan at what he took to be divine prompting, Abraham received a promise from the God he had travelled far to find. He would be the father of a great nation. His descendants would outnumber the stars of heaven or the grains of sand on the seashore.

There was one snag, however. The promise was to him and his wife, Sarah, and she did not get pregnant. As time passed, Abraham turned to a recognised alternative at the time, using his wife's maid, Hagar, as a surrogate mother. She bore him a son, Ishmael. That was good, but not quite what God had promised. The years passed and still Abraham and his wife were childless. A strange encounter with three visitors—angels, it would seem—was to change all that.

The Lord appeared to Abraham by the oaks of Mamre, as he sat at the entrance of his tent in the heat of the day. He looked up and saw three men standing near him. When he saw them, he ran from the tent entrance to meet them, and bowed down to the ground. He said, 'My lord, if I find favour with you, do not pass by your servant. Let a little water be brought, and wash your feet, and rest yourselves under the tree. Let me bring a little bread, that you may refresh yourselves, and after that you may pass on—since you have come to your servant.' So they said, 'Do as you have said.' And Abraham hastened into the tent to Sarah, and said, 'Make ready quickly three measures of choice flour, knead it, and make cakes.' Abraham ran to the herd, and took a calf, tender and good, and gave it to the servant, who hastened to prepare it. Then he took curds and milk and the calf that he had prepared, and set it before them; and he stood by them under the tree while they ate.

They said to him, 'Where is your wife Sarah?' And he said, 'There, in the tent.' Then one said, 'I will surely return to you in due season, and your wife Sarah shall have a son.' And Sarah was listening at the tent entrance behind him. Now Abraham and Sarah were old, advanced in age; it had ceased to be with Sarah after the manner of women. So Sarah laughed to herself, saying, 'After I have grown old, and my husband is old, shall I have pleasure?' The Lord said to Abraham, 'Why did Sarah laugh, and say, "Shall I indeed bear a child, now that I am old?" Is anything too wonderful for the Lord? At the set time I will return to you, in due season, and Sarah shall have a son.'

GENESIS 18:1–14

It's an excellent story and the setting is sketched beautifully. Abraham and his wife, with their family, servants and flocks, have never returned to the city but live the life of nomads. On this warm day, around lunchtime, Abraham is sitting in the shade of the tent flap when three men approach. Throughout the encounter, he seems to treat them as ordinary people, even though they are clearly on a mission of great importance.

Having arranged for a meal to be served for them, Abraham is perhaps surprised to be asked, 'Where is your wife Sarah?' The simple answer is, 'In the tent, making cakes.' Another of the men then says that, in due time, he will return and by then Sarah will have a son.

These words evoked a response from the lady in the tent. She 'laughed to herself' and said, presumably out loud, 'After I have grown old, and my husband is old, shall I have pleasure?' This does not seem to be a response to the idea that she might yet have a son, but is a cry from the heart of someone only too aware of the remorseless march of time. It is 'pleasure' that she speaks of, and—linked with the reference to her husband's age—there's little doubt that she meant sexual pleasure. 'That,' she seems to be saying, 'is a thing of the past for us.'

The man—now described as 'the Lord' (Yahweh)—rebukes Sarah. 'Why did she laugh?' he asks. 'Is anything too wonderful for the Lord?' He then repeats the earlier statement: he will return at the right time, and Sarah will have a son.

The whole story of Sarah, Abraham and his sons is a vital building block in the chronicle of the emergence of Israel as a distinct people. At the time of this visit from the three men, Abraham's first son, Ishmael, had left the family home, Sarah apparently finding his presence (as the son of another woman) unbearable. He would be, in the unfolding story, the 'father' of the Arab nations. Still, however, the promise that Abraham believed he had been given by God remained unfulfilled. The child had been promised to him and Sarah —yet here they were childless, and (as the chronicler delicately puts it) 'it had ceased to be with Sarah after the manner of women' (v. 11). In other words, she had passed the menopause. One might add, from Sarah's comment, that the aged Abraham's fires of passion had perhaps gone out as well.

Abraham, of all the biblical characters, is held up as the prime example of faith in God. That's true from these early narratives right through to the writings of Paul over a millennium later. At the promptings of a God he hardly knew, he had moved from Ur and travelled west, leaving home and kindred in obedience to that inner voice. The same voice had told him, as we have seen, that he would be the father of a mighty nation, through whom all the nations of the earth would be blessed. That was some promise—but where was the promised heir? If Ishmael could not fulfil that role, then the aged Abraham, matched with an aged wife, must have wondered how it could happen. He had been 'told', but had he misunderstood? Could it be that the great patriarch of faith was finding his faith sorely tested?

Then these 'men' appeared. Who were they, these three mysterious visitors? Not surprisingly, the medieval church saw them as 'types' of the Trinity, as depicted in one of the finest and most famous icons, the 'Icon of the Trinity' by Andrei Rublev. They were clearly messengers, which suggests angels—yet one of them speaks directly as the voice of Yahweh, the Lord Almighty. Whoever they were, their message was clear and unambiguous. Sarah would have a son. The promise that Abraham had clung to would be fulfilled.

Sarah

Sarah is in many respects unusual, even unique, among women in the Bible. For one thing, she is the only woman in the whole of the Hebrew and Christian scriptures whose lifespan is recorded: she lived, we are told, for 127 years. She is also one of the few women who seemed able and willing to stand up to the men around her and, very often, get her own way. That was certainly so over the birth, upbringing and eventual dismissal of Ishmael.

Sarah was clearly a character in her own right, as the incident with the three visitors demonstrates, and a woman of passion. We may assume, too, that she was physically attractive, as demonstrated by Abraham's stratagems to deal with powerful men who would otherwise have taken her into their harems (Genesis 12 and 20).

Her death and burial also represent significant landmarks in the unfolding story of the origins of the nation of Israel. It is unwise to pin too much on details in a story that has many editorial complexities, but Jewish commentators have often drawn attention to the fact that her death follows, in the traditional narrative, straight after the highly emotive story of Abraham and Isaac (Genesis 22). Could it be, they wonder, that Abraham's apparent willingness to sacrifice Isaac, the son Sarah had waited for with longing for most of her adult life, was simply too much for her to bear? Did she, as the text seems to imply, at that point leave the marital home and settle, at least temporarily, in Hebron, where she died, while Abraham remained in Beersheba? We read that he 'came to mourn' for her in Hebron (23:2, KJV).

Perhaps that is to read too much into the narrative—or perhaps not. Sarah was evidently a passionate woman, not at all afraid to stand up to her husband when circumstances justified it. Her love for her longed-for son cannot be ignored, nor, perhaps, her difficulty in appreciating the complex ways of God—a difficulty her husband did not seem to feel.

None of that, however, has diminished the respect that Judaism has offered to this remarkable woman, in many ways the chief mother-figure of the religion of Israel. She accompanied Abraham through the long journey of discovery. Eventually ('Is anything too wonderful for the Lord?') her dear son, Isaac, was born. She became in that moment a foundational character in the story of her nation and possibly the reason why, down the ages, 'Jewishness' has been inherited from the mother rather than the father. This was the religion of Abraham, Isaac and Jacob, but throughout its history the women have been essential and respected participants—and Sarah is chief among them.

Is her age important? Yes, surely, and in two respects. Firstly, she was 'old' when she bore Isaac. Disregarding the biological and even historical questions this raises, the chronicler asserts that age was a boon and blessing to the couple, not a curse. Sarah, in her own vivid phrase, could still 'have pleasure' in her age, and from that pleasure could come the second founder figure of Israel—indeed, the man whose own son, Jacob (Israel), gave the nation its name (see Genesis 32:28).

Secondly, Sarah was demonstrably 'alive' to the end of her days—a feisty woman who fought her corner, cared passionately about her husband and her son and became, in life and death, an icon of the traditional Jewish mother. Whatever her actual biological age, it is significant that the scriptures report it as comparable to that of other great figures (such as her husband and even Moses). She was not a woman to take lightly, nor one whose life is to be airbrushed out of the history of the Judeo-Christian tradition.

From the point of view of a book about being old, Sarah is also important because she offers a rare biblical image of a woman in that patriarchal society who seems to have had her own way of 'being old'. Here is no helpless aged woman, dependent on others and, once bereft of her reproductive qualities, no longer fit for purpose. She offers a picture of a positive, life-affirming woman in a society where women tended to be seen simply as wives and child-bearers.

There is also, perhaps, a hint here of a genuine difference between the way men and women tend to experience old age. For women, the great sadness is often in a perceived loss of femininity. The menopause is seen as a kind of frontier that, once crossed, places a woman in another, less rewarding world. For men, on the other hand, the greatest perceived loss is usually that of usefulness. We might wonder whether the distinction (if it exists at all) is created by actual life issues or simply by the way men and women are seen, and see themselves, in modern society.

Moses

Then Moses, the servant of the Lord, died there in the land of Moab, at the Lord's command. He was buried in a valley in the land of Moab, opposite Beth-peor, but no one knows his burial place to this day. Moses was one hundred and twenty years old when he died; his sight was unimpaired and his vigour had not abated.
DEUTERONOMY 34:5–7

I suspect that this description of the aged patriarch Moses will be met with scepticism by many older readers. Like all the patriarchs, he lived to a great age, though not quite the hundreds of years clocked up by the mighty men before the flood. His lifespan, according to the chronicler, was about the same as Abraham and Sarah's, but whereas they showed signs of age ('I have grown old, and my husband is old', Genesis 18:12), here it is claimed that Moses retained his vigour—and his eyesight.

Normally our eyesight begins to deteriorate slightly but progressively from our mid-50s, although it is true that a few people retain remarkably good eyesight into genuine old age. It's the 'vigour' that causes the scepticism. Mental agility may remain, together with artistic and practical skills, but vigour—energy, drive, physical strength—inevitably declines with the passing years. There are no runners in the Olympic Games, for instance, over the age of 50, nor would we expect there to be. No ten-second 100 metres for the octogenarian! As we age, we slow down, as it seems Abraham did.

So why does the writer of Deuteronomy feel the need to make this particular claim for Moses? We've seen already that length of days was regarded in the ancient world as a sign of God's blessing, life itself being a gift of God. Now, with this seminal figure in the history of the Jewish people, the writer is making a further point. The gift of God is not simply duration but also quality of life. Moses was the uniquely chosen and divinely endowed leader of the liberation of Israel from slavery in Egypt. Therefore, as the chronicler sees it, he was rewarded by God both with length of days and quality of life. There may have been a collective memory that Moses retained many powers into old age, but just as we might not take the duration of his life literally, we need not take literally the claim about his eyesight and vigour. That claim was not necessarily validated by historical or factual accuracy but by the God-given status of Moses, the patriarch.

Quality of life

We are probably all familiar with the phrase 'quality of life' and it is frequently used in relation to ageing. We have applied it here to the life of the old man Moses. An old person with a clear mind and a degree of mobility is described as having 'quality of life'. Conversely, someone with advanced dementia or a crippling progressive condition, such as motor neurone disease, is said to lack it. In the continuing debate about end-of-life issues, 'quality' rather than 'quantity' is increasingly becoming a determining factor. There are many who would argue that if life has lost any 'quality' (variously defined) then it might as well be brought to an end.

In this brief resumé of the final stages of the life of Moses, the writer is concerned to make the point that he wasn't just 'old' but alert and vigorous, and this was itself a sign of blessing. I suppose we too might regard continuing alertness and vigour as a 'blessing'. The problem comes when we view the reverse situation. If an old person lacks mental clarity or physical vigour, is it evidence that his or her life is no longer worth living?

The trouble here is that 'worth living' is a loaded phrase. Generally speaking, it tends to mean a life that is pleasurable, fulfilling and meaningful. We test life, then, by the norms of earlier experience: can the old person think clearly, make intelligent decisions, and recognise and enjoy company, family and friends? If not, it is very easy to decide—generally on behalf of someone else—that their life is not 'worth living'.

This issue is distinct from questions of pain and acute physical or mental incapacity, of course. Most of us would agree that levels of pain and physical distress can reach a point at which they are literally intolerable, when palliative care may necessarily have the secondary effect of shortening life. This is not at all the same as a value judgment about 'quality of life', especially when it is made by someone other than the person who is actually experiencing that life.

Every elderly person—indeed, all of us who are approaching, even distantly, the evening years of life—is aware that powers normally decline with age. Ecclesiastes paints a picture that we can recognise. Conversely, the chronicler's picture of old Moses sounds too good to be credible. Most of us would not expect to reach old age with our eyesight undimmed and our vigour unabated. Into our thinking and even planning for old age we factor that gradual diminution of powers. At the same time, we can easily distinguish between sheer longevity (which may or may not be an unmixed blessing) and a peaceful and fulfilling evening of life. We know in our hearts that life is judged not by how long it is but by how good it is.

It may well be that the chronicler of the death of Moses was making the point simply that he had lived a rich and fulfilling life—not fault-free, but in constant communion with God—and that its richness and fulfilment were genuinely and literally lifelong. Whatever the state of our eyesight or the vigour of our bodies, that may be true for every one of us.

From birth to old age

As we have seen, the birth of a famous person in distant days was often presented as having been a remarkable or even miraculous event—so the woman had been 'barren' and the man very old, yet between them they had become the parents of this great leader, prophet or patriarch. There have always been unexpected and remarkable births and perhaps those born in such circumstances start with an advantage over the rest of us: they know they are 'special'.

It's not only the Bible that records such births, either. Ancient history is full of them: Julius Caesar was (in Shakespeare's phrase) 'from his mother's womb untimely ripped'. His birth became the name of a medical procedure, 'Caesarean section', which has saved the lives of many babies (even though, until modern times, usually causing the death of their mothers).

However, it is the Bible's stories that are most familiar: Isaac, Moses, Samuel, John the Baptist and, most memorable of all, Jesus himself. In different ways, their births marked them out as predestined for a major role in the unfolding story of salvation, which is the Bible's core narrative. The importance of their birth narratives, therefore, is primarily theological, not medical or historical. God's hand was on these people from the womb—or, in the case of Jesus, even before that.

So birth was significant as a sign of potential greatness. Old age, on the other hand, was a sign of greatness achieved and recognised. In both cases, the biblical narratives endorse the events with special signs. 'Look out for this child,' they seem to say; 'he or she is marked out for great things in God's purposes.' Honour this man or woman of great age, for they have earned the accolade of long life.

Consequently, as we have already seen, old people were not regarded as 'problems' but as signs of blessing. As Ecclesiastes points out, they will experience physical decline but it is to be matched by spiritual honour. Significantly, the only one of the Ten Commandments that makes a specific promise to those who keep it is the one about 'honouring' fathers and mothers. Those who do so will, it says, live 'long in the land' (Exodus 20:12). Not surprisingly, therefore, Jewish family life right down the ages has experienced little problem with age. Elderly people are still members of the family, honoured by their children and grandchildren. Even in the contemporary setting, it is noticeable that the extended family remains a powerful glue holding the Jewish community together.

Of course it is simplistic to offer this as a solution to all the problems surrounding old age. Even the most faithful Jewish family, faced with an elderly member suffering from advanced dementia, will probably not be able to cope with them at home permanently. Twenty-four hour care makes enormous demands of love and understanding and, for many practical reasons—housing, finance, employment and health—it sometimes brings even the most dedicated carer to breaking point.

I do not think that 'honour' in this commandment requires any specific duty of care so much as an attitude of respect and love. Perhaps these scriptural stories of the old illustrate for us something of that attitude. However far-fetched we may find the details, the emerging story is one of respect and honour for old age, and that must surely be the key factor for any society in its treatment of the elderly.

In practice, this generally is the case. The media may give us the impression that the elderly are unwanted and unloved, but in the great majority of families that is a distortion of the truth. In pastoral ministry, I've been moved time and again to see the love that marks the relationship between a son or daughter (themselves perhaps no longer young) and an elderly parent. That love is not diminished by the effects of age—rather the contrary. Just as babies, in their vulnerability, evoke tender care, so (it seems to me) does the vulnerability of parents who are no longer able to care for themselves. One can see in the eyes of the younger generation treasured memories of bygone days and a deep gratitude for the love and care they received in the past from the one for whom they now, in their turn, are privileged to care.

'Honour your father and your mother'. Not for the last time, we shall see that profound truths about being old are to be found in the ancient wellsprings of human experience and wisdom.

5

Staying fresh and green

In old age they still produce fruit; they are always green and full of sap.

PSALM 92:14

Who are they, these ever-productive old people positively bursting with 'sap'? According to the psalmist, they are the 'righteous', which in biblical code means those who do what God requires, who seek to live by his laws and precepts. That's not, according to the longest psalm in the Bible (Psalm 119), simply a matter of buckling down and keeping the rules, but a positive and rewarding way of life. Indeed, those who meditate on God's decrees 'understand more than the aged' (119:100), which is an interesting comment in the light of the verse above.

I suspect that the writer was speaking with a prophetic voice rather than describing the actual circumstances of old people, even those who were 'righteous'. I know scores of old people who have sought to live in faith and obedience who, sadly, could not be described as 'green and full of sap'. Some are, some aren't, just as some teenagers are awkward and some delightful, even though the teenage years are invariably characterised as difficult, even tempestuous. The psalmist is describing the ideal, a vision of an evening of life marked by 'fruitfulness' and a rich enjoyment of days. Both are not only possible (health permitting) but also, I would suggest, more common than television documentaries and even social surveys suggest.

Fruitfulness is an interesting concept. It evokes visions of heavily laden apple trees or cherries hanging in great bunches on their boughs. It speaks of something internal—life, 'sap'—finding expression in something external and valuable. In terms of old age, that 'fruit' can be seen in a grandparent's love, in prayer that embraces the needs of family, friends and neighbours, in small but loving deeds of kindness and in a smiling and friendly face in the local supermarket. If anyone thinks these are trivial examples of 'fruitfulness', then they have not understood what it means to be truly human.

This definition of fruitfulness can properly include all those old people who are willing and able to be its agents. Affection, care, family love, cheerfulness and especially prayer are within the compass of almost every one of us. They don't require mobility or even freedom from aches and pains. They don't demand brilliant hearing or 20/20 eyesight. They are the fruit of a quiet and contented heart, and my feeling is that such a heart is surprisingly more common among the elderly than we might suppose. I think it is the explanation of the profound love that most grandchildren have for their grandparents. The eyes of youth quickly detect insincerity or fakery. They can often recognise in their grandparents a serenity and contentment acquired through the experience of the long and winding journey of life.

Fruitfulness in old age can, of course, extend beyond matters of character, disposition and attitude. For instance, many natural gifts and acquired skills survive largely untouched by the onset of age. I have a friend who is a distinguished potter and his hands seem as skilful at the wheel today as they were 60 years ago. Playing a musical instrument, painting, horticulture—these are skills in which any decline in performance is more than offset by the gains of experience.

As a writer, I've found that although the exact word (what the French call 'le mot juste') sometimes takes a little longer to surface, I have learnt not to worry but to press on. It will pop up like an old friend eventually, and one of the blessings of the computer is that it's easily inserted in its rightful place. Writing, in fact, is a skill (or gift) largely unhampered by old age. My great heroine P.D. James—president of the Society of Authors and distinguished writer of scores of crime novels—is still producing ingenious and elegant books in her 90s, and she is not alone. George Bernard Shaw wrote into his tenth decade and so, on a very different literary level, did Barbara Cartland.

Perhaps more to the point for most of us, who are not world-famous authors or playwrights, is that it's perfectly possible for older people to find much fulfilment in writing at a more personal level. We can write up our memoirs, not necessarily for publication but as living testimonies to our descendants. The exercise is, in itself, an enjoyable and rewarding one and, in the process, some have found (as my own mother did) a genuine talent that had lain dormant through 60 years.

Serenity

One of the keys to fruitfulness in old age is, as has already been suggested, serenity—a calm, peaceful and tranquil approach to life. It is true, I confess, that the old can be touchy. The Angry Old Man and his female equivalent are not simply products of fiction. We exist (and I shall come to that subject later in this chapter) but so does the serene old person—and often in the self-same body. At its best, serenity is the most attractive feature of the elderly, the product of a wiser evaluation of priorities and a lifelong experience of ups and downs.

We who sit in the departure lounge of life know deep down that much of what people worry about (and what we ourselves have wasted precious years worrying about) is really pretty trivial. It takes the watery eyes of the old to see that the football results, the empty shelf where our favourite fruit should be at the supermarket or the failed MOT on the car are not apocalyptic events but passing moments in a constantly moving kaleidoscope of life. Serenity comes with knowledge, and knowledge, in this respect at least, comes through experience of life. That funny slogan from the war years, 'Keep calm and carry on' captures the feeling exactly.

You may well enquire at exactly what moment in life this precious gift of serenity emerges, and there is no precise answer. For me, it's still emerging, I hope—but I know scores of old people who are quite extraordinarily immune to fuss, panic, anger or petulance. For some, it came as they laid aside earlier ambitions and settled for what they had. For others, it was an acquired gift, slowly cultivated over a period of years, as they reassessed priorities and began to decide what was truly important and what wasn't.

The apostle Paul, when he was a decade or so short of being 'old', made a remarkable claim: 'I have learned to be content with whatever I have. I know what it is to have little, and I know what it is to have plenty. In any and all circumstances I have learned the secret of being well-fed and of going hungry, of having plenty and of being in need' (Philippians 4:11–12).

For me, the interesting and challenging word there is 'learned'. In an extraordinarily difficult and perilous life, with scores of issues that he could justifiably have worried about, the apostle was 'learning' contentment and serenity. Perhaps it was the very experience of anxiety, pressure, demands on his time and obstacles in his way that led him to search for it, to learn the message of inward peace and tranquillity.

It has to be said that even a quick reading of his letters and the Acts of the Apostles suggests that serenity would not have come easily to this man. There was not a lot of it around when he argued fiercely with his fellow apostle Peter (Galatians 2:11–14) or when he shouted at the high priest, 'God will strike you, you whitewashed wall!' (Acts 23:3). In a way, that is reassuring, because it tells us that the gift of serenity is not only for the characteristically calm and composed but also (if 'learned') for those of a more combustible temperament. 'Learned' also tells us that it is the end of a process, and sometimes that process may take a lifetime.

Full of sap

Perhaps, then, we can understand how the lives of the elderly may be fruitful, but what about 'full of sap'? What on earth does that mean in practice—or is it just a poetic phrase that the psalmist added to make up the line (all amateur poets know the feeling)? 'Sap' is an interesting word. It describes the fluid—made up mostly of water and nutrients—that flows through the vascular system of plants. Without it, the plant would perish, literally starved of its essential nourishment. In a land where livelihood and survival depended on the growth and health of plants—vines, fig trees, wheat, corn and fruit— the people of Israel would have known the essential function of sap and what it meant to say that some old people could be full of it.

Sap gives life. It flows through the plant's interior systems and nourishes it. Indeed, without being too fanciful, we could say that the sap does not exist for itself but solely to nourish the plant. That is an intriguing image to use of an old man or woman. In what way could they be said to nourish and nurture life in others?

Sap is usually associated with energy and vigour, two qualities that tend to diminish with increasing age, but the old are often remarkably good at nurturing vigour and energy in others. Just watch a grandparent talking to a grandchild about books, films or plays. What is actually happening is that their own lifelong enthusiasm is being transferred, by a kind of osmosis, to the next-but-one generation. The intriguing fact is that youngsters will often accept that transfusion from a grandparent while resisting it from a parent. The sap of enthusiasm is a most precious commodity, and often no one is better placed to provide it than an elderly relative or friend.

I have said that energy and vigour inevitably diminish with age, and that is true of physical strength. I gave up playing hockey seriously when I was 33, 'feeling my age'. Now, nearly 50 years later, two minutes kicking a ball in the garden with my teenage grandson sends me breathless to a comfortable sofa to recover.

Mental energy and vigour

Physical strength is not, however, the only measure of energy and vigour. I watched an 85-year-old clergy veteran leading a lively harvest service in a packed country church, and what struck me most was the energy that he put into it. He related wonderfully to the many children present, probably because they saw in him their own grandparents (or even great-grandparents). There was laughter, but there was also an experienced hand on the tiller and the service never degenerated into chaos.

Mental energy and vigour can and usually do survive the reduction of physical strength. I visited a friend, a retired clergyman, not long after he had celebrated his 100th birthday. At the party, he had delivered a brief homily based on a verse in the Gospel story of Jesus turning water into wine. When the 'new wine' was brought to the master of ceremonies, he remarked, 'You have kept the good wine until now' (John 2:10), and my friend took that as his text. Far from feeling sorry for himself or apologising for his physical weakness or tired old body, he celebrated the life that he still had, surrounded, on that occasion, by scores of friends (and his bishop).

He was more or less immobile and he looked physically frail, but he had saved up a whole list of questions for my visit. He wanted to know my views on current theological, ethical and scientific issues. I was hopeless on the last-named, but he had a science degree (earned in the 1930s) and had kept up with developments in that field, too. Half an hour of cross-examination by this feisty centenarian was enough to dispel any notion on my part that mental vigour was declining. A few weeks later, however, the fate spelt out in Ecclesiastes befell him: the silver cord broke, the frail body returned to the dust and his spirit to the God who created it. Yet what I remembered most of all was that astonishing mental vigour, right to the end.

Listeners to Radio 4's *Today* programme may remember an interview in 2011 in which the Director-General of the BBC was grilled by the novelist and former BBC Governor Baroness James (P.D. James, to whom I have already referred).

So rigorous was her questioning, so wide her research and so quick her response to evasive answers, that the interview won an annual press award. At the time, she had just reached 90 years of age. No lack of 'vigour or energy' there!

Of course, these are exceptional examples. Generally speaking, the brain as well as the body tends to slow down with age. Experience, however, makes up for many failings, and so does a well-preserved intelligence. Use is probably the key: those who have never stopped using their mental faculties to the full seem less likely to see their early decline.

Contrary characteristics

It's only fair, in discussing old people who are 'fruitful' and 'full of sap', to accept that old age can bring, or at least exacerbate, contrary characteristics. When an elderly parent, for instance, becomes unreasonably demanding, frequently angry (usually with those closest to hand, which may well be a daughter or other family member) or bitter and ungrateful, it is not just painful for those on the receiving end, souring the relationship and turning every day into a domestic battle field. It is also profoundly sad and destructive for the old person involved. It's in circumstances like these that it becomes difficult, or even impossible, to continue to provide daily or other regular care for the old person.

Sometimes what happens is that negative characteristics, which have been present but hidden by the requirements of a civilised relationship, begin to emerge in old age. No longer held back by the need to be polite, let alone grateful, minor resentments that have smouldered for decades may begin to emerge in angry words and thoughtless accusations. The veneer that we construct to hide our less attractive characteristics wears thin and may disappear altogether. This is a behavioural issue, very much like the tantrums of a two-year-old—but you can't put Grandpa on the naughty stair.

Sometimes, however, the cause is psychiatric. The elderly mother or father is not being abusive or cruel by choice, but is driven by strange and frightening changes in their brain. To recognise this fact may reduce the hurt for other members of the family, but it doesn't solve the problem of care. 'Honouring my parents' does not necessarily mean day-and-night care for the rest of their lives, certainly not when my very presence seems to upset them profoundly. This is one of the most distressing aspects of old age—when positive and lifelong love is tested by the onset of dementia. At some point, even the most loving children may have to accept that they cannot provide the kind of long-term care that an elderly parent needs.

The tantrums of the terrible 80s

That is how observers see the awkward and cantankerous old, those who are simply behaving badly and those whose behaviour is shaped by illness. This book, however, is not about neutral observation or medical diagnosis. It's not even simply about other people being old; it's about me being old. So can this particular old man shed any light on the tantrums of the terrible 80s?

The awful truth is that I can—and so, I suspect, can many old people. As I've claimed, many people acquire a glorious serenity in old age. Sadly, for others, something seems to happen to tolerance as they enter the departure hall of life. I confess that I am one of them. Petty irritations, which once I would have laughed off, become incredibly upsetting. There's no excuse for it. Simply pleading that I'm old doesn't excuse impatience, irritation, even fits of something approaching blind rage.

It's an observable phenomenon, which we've mentioned already—the 'Grumpy Old Man or Woman' syndrome. It's relatively harmless while the rage is directed at modern follies or the futility of automatic machines or the grammatical lapses of broadcasters, all of which, in the right circumstances, can induce a tantrum in this particular senior citizen.

It's not harmless, however, when that childish temper is vented on the woman in front of me in the supermarket queue, simply because at the very moment when the cashier had put all the items through the till, she remembered that she should have bought a tin of baked beans and scurried off to find them. On this occasion, the pleasant, smiley Christian that I profess to be suddenly became curt, rude, even sarcastic. I greeted her eventual return with 'Are you sure you haven't forgotten the sausages?' My excuse for it? Hard to say. I wasn't in a particular hurry. I'd done it myself, several times, and the offending lady was apologising profusely. I collected my goods and, five minutes later, realised how stunningly unpleasant and, yes, childish I had been. On a bad day I excuse it on the grounds that I'm old and tetchy, so there.

Morally responsible
I have to face the fact that rudeness, cruel words and actions, sarcasm and all the other verbal weapons in the human armoury are not excusable simply on grounds of age. Moral responsibility doesn't cease with the arrival of a pension or an 80th birthday. Cruel and unkind words, particularly when addressed to someone we love, are as sinful when spoken by an octogenarian as when uttered by a 30-year-old. We are not suddenly in a different moral world, where we are free to

hurt and wound without apology or penitence. If that were so, then we would be less than fully human, because making moral and ethical decisions and being responsible for their consequences is the surest sign of our being made in the image of God

I suspect that younger people—middle-aged sons and daughters, very often—who are the objects of elderly intolerance put up with it, or even excuse it, more readily than they should. My daughter once gently rebuked me when I had got into a tizzy while waiting at a railway level crossing. She was right, and I took the point. To get angry at an unavoidable event—one over which I had no control—was both pointless and needlessly upsetting. No matter how much I raged, those barriers would not go up one second sooner. Meanwhile, I had raised my blood pressure for no good reason and revealed to my grandchildren on the back seat that I could be as childish as they had once been (but had now grown out of). It does not help the elderly offender if, out of misguided 'respect' for age or a desire to keep the peace at all costs, those who are best placed to do so fail to register any kind of rebuke or correction. In fact, true love demands it.

None of this applies, of course, where the angry words are the products of dementia or of extreme pain or intolerable circumstances. My own view, held tentatively, is that withdrawal is often the best response. Trained professional staff are less likely to be hurt, even deeply wounded, by words that they recognise as arising from circumstances the patient cannot control. A regular visit may be a better answer than a fruitless attempt at 24/7 care.

Still fruitful and full of sap?

All of these thoughts were prompted by the psalmist's description of the 'righteous', even in old age, still producing fruit and being 'always green and full of sap'. It's a beautiful image, one well worth cherishing for ourselves and the people we care for. It is not, however, and cannot be, a description of the destiny of every old person. I like to think of it as a glorious ideal—an ideal that we can sometimes see fulfilled in a serene, positive and outward-looking old age.

If, for us or someone we love, the fruit is less than luscious and the sap somewhat dried up, we can still celebrate the ideal and pray that the Lord of the years, who holds the whole of life in his hands, will nurture what there is. Even for the truly old, nothing is beyond redemption and no situation is irretrievably hopeless.

Perhaps we can echo Robert Browning's 'Rabbi Ben Ezra' (1864):

Grow old along with me!
The best is yet to be,
The last of life, for which the first was made:
Our times are in his hand
Who saith 'A whole I planned,
Youth shows but half; trust God: see all nor be afraid!'

6

Living and waiting

Now there was a man in Jerusalem whose name was Simeon; this man was righteous and devout, looking forward to the consolation of Israel, and the Holy Spirit rested on him. It had been revealed to him by the Holy Spirit that he would not see death before he had seen the Lord's Messiah. Guided by the Spirit, Simeon came into the temple; and when the parents brought in the child Jesus, to do for him what was customary under the law, Simeon took him in his arms and praised God, saying, 'Master, now you are dismissing your servant in peace, according to your word; for my eyes have seen your salvation, which you have prepared in the presence of all peoples, a light for revelation to the Gentiles and for glory to your people Israel.'...

There was also a prophet, Anna the daughter of Phanuel, of the tribe of Asher. She was of a great age, having lived with her husband for seven years after her marriage, then as a widow to the age of eighty-four. She never left the temple but worshipped there with fasting and prayer night and day. At that moment she came, and began to praise God and to speak about the child to all who were looking for the redemption of Jerusalem.

LUKE 2:25–32, 36–38

'Why do you go on writing?' someone asked me. I mentally sorted through the 20 or so answers that I have available, and chose the one I usually reserve for anyone I judge to be incapable of understanding the drivenness of the long-distance author. 'It gives me a reason to get up in the morning,' I said. He seemed satisfied, while nurturing, I fear, a picture of me still in bed at noon, dirty cups unwashed and yesterday's stubble still on my face.

It's a truthful answer, if probably the least compelling of the 20. Life needs a purpose or it's simply a kind of ramble through the years (and I have never seen the point of rambling). Most people live for something. It may be noble, like the pilgrimage of faith, or pleasurable, like crosswords or carpet bowls, or rewarding, like pottery or painting—or writing. To live without purpose is to drift from day to day.

In the colourful story from Luke's Gospel above, we meet two old people who were certainly living with purpose. Their purpose, however, was to 'wait'. That may not seem a very 'purposeful' thing to do but in their case it absorbed all their devotion.

Simeon was an old man who had been 'told' by the Holy Spirit that he wouldn't die until he had seen the Messiah. That might have seemed rather a long shot, because the people of Israel had already been 'waiting' for the event for well over a thousand years. Still, Simeon—'righteous and devout'— waited and prayed until the moment when, prompted by the Holy Spirit, he came into the temple to see two parents with a young child arriving for the rite of purification. This, he realised, was the moment. He took the child in his arms, declaring to the parents and the watching crowd that his eyes had now seen God's 'salvation'.

Among those watching was Anna, who was probably a well-known character to temple-goers, because she never left its precincts, 'fasting and praying day and night'. Aged 84, she is described by Luke as 'of a great age'—though positively youthful compared to Methuselah or even Abraham, Sarah and Moses. However, her description probably reflects the factual position rather more realistically. Luke describes her as a 'prophet', of the tribe of Asher, and she was 'looking for the redemption of Israel'. Her days were spent in the temple, in expectant prayer. So they both 'waited', this contrasting elderly couple, until the moment came.

Ways of waiting

All through life we seem to be waiting, in the everyday sense of the word. The child waits for schooldays or to be a teenager. The young adult waits to find a partner, then they wait to have a family. Later, in middle age, many people wait impatiently for retirement. After that, believe it or not, there's still more waiting to do, including waiting for the final moment of translation into whatever lies beyond the experience we call death.

Much of this waiting is entirely passive, like waiting for a bus or train. We can't make the expected event come any sooner and we have to face the fact that it may not come at all: 'First Great Western regrets that the 9:58 to Paddington has been cancelled.' Waiting tests patience, but it also stretches out our pleasures. It includes the strange joy of anticipation, the 'waiting for Christmas' excitement that we can remember from childhood.

When the Bible speaks of 'waiting', however, the word often carries a much more profound and less passive meaning. The psalms often speak of 'waiting for the Lord' and they definitely don't mean doing nothing. Waiting, in this sense, is related to watching. 'As the eyes of servants look to the hand of their master, as the eyes of a maid to the hand of her mistress, so our eyes look to the Lord our God, until he has mercy upon us' (Psalm 123:2). These 'servants' are certainly 'waiting' ('until he has mercy') but their waiting is not passive. Their eyes are fixed on the hands of the master or mistress, waiting for a sign to which they must respond.

They are not unlike the watchmen on the walls of the city in another psalm: 'I wait for the Lord, my soul waits, and in his word I hope; my soul waits for the Lord more than those who watch for the morning, more than those who watch for the morning' (130:5–6). The comparison here is intriguing: 'I wait for the Lord more than those who watch for the morning.' There doesn't immediately seem to be any logical connection.

'Waiting' usually implies the obedient, patient watchfulness exemplified by the servants in Psalm 123. We 'wait' for him so as to know what he wishes us to do. But the watchmen on the walls of the city seem to be engaged in a very different occupation.

In ancient times, watchmen stood on the ramparts to guard the city during the night and to watch, eagle-eyed, for the first rays of the sun topping the eastern horizon in the morning. When it happened, they roused the citizens: the day had begun. There was no time to waste; daylight was short and sunset early. Once their cry was heard, the streets would fill, the markets be set up and the wagons creak off with their loads, out of the city gates.

It was the cry of the watchmen that caused this sudden burst of early morning activity. They had watched the eastern sky, waiting for dawn. They knew it would come; it always did. They even knew roughly when—but their task was to wait, watch and then instigate action. It was not a spectator sport. They were not lounging in deckchairs to watch the sunrise in all its glory. They were there for a purpose, and that purpose was to respond to the moment. Like Simeon and Anna, the watchmen and the servants in the earlier psalm had a reactive, not passive, task. They waited patiently, and then, at the right moment, a greater purpose would be fulfilled.

In the case of Simeon and Anna in the temple, that was the greatest of all purposes. In their old age, after long years of waiting, they had seen the promised Saviour, 'a light for revelation to the Gentiles and for glory to your people Israel'. Standing there in the temple courts, they were able to bear witness to the most astonishing event in human history—the incarnation. God had taken the initiative and come to them in this tiny child.

Nothing more to do

No wonder Simeon felt that there was nothing left for him to do. His eyes had seen the glory and he was now ready to leave the stage: 'Master, now you are dismissing your servant in peace, according to your word; for my eyes have seen your salvation.' Anna had words for the watching crowd—and we can imagine that the crowd was large and excited by now. She praised God and spoke to the bystanders about the redemption of God's people that this child would bring about.

And then they left. We hear no more of them, possibly because, having climbed the mountain, they were now in the promised land. The event for which they had waited had occurred, and it would be the task of others, like the watchmen on the ramparts, to turn the dawn they had announced into a day of fulfilment. As another old man, Zechariah, the father of John the Baptist, put it, 'By the tender mercy of our God, the dawn from on high will break upon us, to give light to those who sit in darkness and in the shadow of death, to guide our feet into the way of peace' (Acts 1:78–79).

Rage or repose

Among my octogenarian friends and contemporaries, there is a quite clear divide, although most of us sometimes veer from one side of it to the other. As we have seen, some become quite irrationally angry about relatively minor things— modern manners, changes in church, even the layout of the local supermarket. They can get very uptight about the BBC (and, even more, ITV). They can rage against personalities they have never met, honest and upright citizens who have invoked their ire on television or on the radio. They tend to see the world as a conspiracy of mindless change, all designed to make their lives more frustrating and irritating.

And, yes, as I have already confessed, I have joined their ranks from time to time. Sometimes I will spend an entertaining hour with a contemporary simply railing at the stupidities of the modern world. Things were not like this in our young days! It's not hard to find fuel for the fire and, at the end, as we part, we feel a certain satisfaction that we, at least, are not willing collaborators in the crazy world around us. Mind you, we go home to text our friends with our views, put them on Facebook and email them at greater length to those we deem worthy of it. Our indignation is nothing if not selective.

On the other side, there are those who, at the same stage of life, seem to have acquired an almost mystical serenity, a deep patience that declines to allow the passing issues of the day to disturb its peace. They are not always deeply religious; they are not necessarily even churchgoers. Yet something in their inner being has invoked a sense of perspective that allows them to see railway delays, road closures, an irritating voice on television or a neighbour who will place his wheelie bin where theirs should be as trivial and irrelevant distractions from the business of being and living. Again, just occasionally (far too infrequently), I have also joined their ranks.

I have a long-standing friend with an incurable medical condition who has discovered in the evening of his life this kind of tranquillity. I deeply envy him. He owes it, he claims, to the Quaker discipline of silence. Every day he sets aside half an hour—the most rewarding time of the day, he says— when he reads his Bible, says a few prayers and then simply maintains silence. In that silence he discovers the strength and patience to deal with all that has happened, and will yet happen, in his life. I know him as well as I know anybody and I can testify that the change in him is profound. He has learnt to watch and wait.

Watching and waiting

As we get old, we can either rail against the inevitable, fight to hold back the toll of the years and get frustrated and angry at what is going on around us as well as in our own lives, or we can 'watch and wait'. As we have seen, that is not necessarily a passive response. Those who 'watch' are waiting so that, like Simeon, Anna and the watchmen on the city walls, they can be part of a positive response to what lies ahead.

For the old, what lies ahead is both known and unknown. Part of it, like the dawn, is unavoidable. We know the end of the story, and part of that watching and waiting is inevitably focused on death. Much of what lies ahead, however, is still unknown—family, friends, interests, events. The teenager waits expectantly for the end-of-term Prom. The old person waits expectantly for a granddaughter's marriage or a fifth grandchild or great-grandchild, or a nephew's graduation. I honestly think we have the better of it!

A particular gift

For the elderly, the future is obviously limited. We're not going to run a four-minute mile or score the winning goal at Wembley. We're not likely to be cast as Romeo or Juliet in the local dramatic production. Yet for many of us there are achievable goals, which are not wrong to cherish as possibilities. For the artist, potter or poet, there may still be another moment of sublime creativity. For the gardener, green fingers may yet again bring to life a thing of utter beauty. For the organist, those aged fingers may yet strike the glorious Lost Chord.

At a different level, the elderly can very often be excellent hosts—cooks, even—at events that friends will enjoy and remember. For one thing, they're less likely to worry about what kind of impression they're making or whether the menu they have chosen is currently fashionable. One of the best dinner parties I have enjoyed for years included, as the main course, toad in the hole—not a common item on the *Masterchef* menu.

On top of that, there is the wonderful possibility of nurturing gifts and achievement in the younger generation—our grandchildren, nephews and nieces—as we encourage them to develop their own God-given talents.

Watching and waiting seems to be a particular gift for the

old—the patience to wait and the faith to act on what we see, to become part of the divine purpose for ourselves and others. It's a high calling, as Simeon and Anna found long ago, but it brought them joy and fulfilment, as it has done for many an old soul down the long ages.

7

Across the generations

One of my most vivid childhood memories is of playing in the road in our remote Welsh village and constantly dodging to avoid old people in groups of twos or threes engaged in endless conversations. What on earth did they find to talk about at such length, I wondered. And why was it only the old—*henoed*, in Welsh—who did it?

I know now, on both counts. There is never any shortage of conversational material for those who are old. Our heads are stored with it. It may be recollections of time past ('Remember how old Owen Pencoed used to kill his chickens—one twist and they were gone!') or gossip about the present ('Have you heard that the Jones girl is pregnant again?'). For us modern oldies, it may be dire warnings about what will happen if 'something isn't done about it', the 'it' varying from the small roundabout near the pet shop to the misbehaviour of young men and women around the kebab stall in the marketplace of an evening. Scratch us and we have an opinion. Scratch deeper and we have a manifesto. Talk? We can do it for hours.

So the first question is easy. The well of elderly conversation never dries up. The second is slightly harder. Why only the old? The simple answer, in those war-time years, was that only the elderly, and a few women with large families, were around during daylight hours. The others were working either on the land or, in the towns, in shops or factories.

This simple answer won't stand up to further scrutiny, however, because now, in our liberated modern world, it is still true that people tend to gather in their own age groups. On the whole, we prefer to spend time with our contemporaries, because theirs is the country we know and, for the old, so much of today's world is like a foreign land where we don't know the language. You can see it in the Women's Institute (mostly women past retirement age, in many branches), the Mothers' Union (in practice a Grandmothers' Union) and in the Royal British Legion. In one village where I lived, the best-supported group was the 'Good Companions', but you had to be past 60 to join. Saga Holidays confirm the point: 'Nobody under 55' is their unique selling point. On the whole, and with exceptions, we are at our most relaxed with people of our own generation.

Those exceptions are, however, highly significant. Most older people enjoy the company of their own children and grandchildren and relate to them warmly and enthusiastically. Many of us have friends who are much younger: I would count three or four people who are 20 or more years younger than I am as very close friends. Building bridges across the generation gaps is one way of staying in touch with life. It is an enriching experience both for the old and the young—a kind of dialogue of understanding.

Using the biblical spreadsheet once again, it's possible to find several examples from these ancient texts of the positive value and rich rewards to be gained from building personal bridges across the dividing years. They can stand as models of an experience that enriches both youth and age.

Eli and Samuel

Samuel was ministering before the Lord, a boy wearing a linen ephod. His mother used to make for him a little robe and take it to him each year, when she went up with her husband to offer the yearly sacrifice. Then Eli would bless Elkanah and his wife, and say, 'May the Lord repay you with children by this woman for the gift that she made to the Lord'; and then they would return to their home...

Now the boy Samuel was ministering to the Lord under Eli. The word of the Lord was rare in those days; visions were not widespread. At that time Eli, whose eyesight had begun to grow dim so that he could not see, was lying down in his room; the lamp of God had not yet gone out, and Samuel was lying down in the temple of the Lord, where the ark of God was. Then the Lord called, 'Samuel! Samuel!' and he said, 'Here I am!' and ran to Eli, and said, 'Here I am, for you called me.' But he said, 'I did not call; lie down again.' So he went and lay down. The Lord called again, 'Samuel!' Samuel got up and went to Eli, and said, 'Here I am, for you called me.' But he said, 'I did not call, my son; lie down again.' ... The Lord called Samuel again, a third time. And he got up and went to Eli, and said, 'Here I am, for you called me.' Then Eli perceived that the Lord was calling the boy. Therefore Eli said to Samuel, 'Go, lie down; and if he calls you, you shall say, "Speak, Lord, for your servant is listening."'

1 SAMUEL 2:18–20; 3:1–6, 8–9

As a kind of prologue to the eventual anointing of the first king of Israel, we have this intimate story of a young boy and an old man. Samuel was the child of Hannah and Elkanah. Hannah had been unable to bear children, but, on a visit to the house of the Lord at Shiloh, she had met the priest

Eli and vowed that if she had a son he would be dedicated to God from birth. Eli had prayed that her longing and her promise would be fulfilled, and in due course she had a baby son, Samuel. In fulfilment of her vow, as soon as he was weaned (in those days, probably at about 18 months or two years), she brought him to Eli and the child grew up under the care of the temple servants.

Each year, as we've read, Elkanah and Hannah visited the shrine to bring an offering and to see their son as he grew up. Time passed, with young Samuel now probably fulfilling several roles in the worship and life of the temple: one commentator has compared his life to that of a choirboy in an Anglican cathedral! Eventually, perhaps when he was about 12, he seems to have been given the responsibility of assisting Eli, who by now was frail and blind. He slept near the old man and clearly there was a warmth and mutual respect in their relationship.

In modern welfare jargon, Samuel was effectively Eli's 'carer'. We know that a surprisingly high number of children of school age in Britain fulfil that role today, sometimes for a disabled parent, sometimes for an elderly grandparent living in the family home. While other youngsters go out to play, they come home from school to make tea and help with hygiene and medication issues. Samuel, like many such children, was probably old beyond his years. Certainly the events related in these opening chapters of 1 Samuel would have demanded of him a remarkable degree of maturity.

Eli was a holy man but weak, it was alleged, in his control of his sons, who were abusing the sanctity of the temple by fraud and by demanding sexual favours from the women who 'served at the entrance of the tent of meeting' (1 Samuel 2:22). The reputation of the temple and the worship of God

were at stake and so divine intervention was to take place. Eli
had been privately warned by 'a man of God' about his sons'
activities (v. 27), but he still seemed unable to do anything
to stop them.

A voice in the night

One night, young Samuel was sleeping near the ark of the
Lord when he became aware of a voice calling him. Assuming
it was Eli (which would have been normal), he went to
the old man and said, 'You called me.' Eli told him that he
hadn't and sent him back to bed, but twice more Samuel was
awoken by the voice. On the third occasion, Eli recognised
that something unusual was happening. He told the boy that
if he heard the voice again, he was to say, 'Speak, Lord, for
your servant is listening.'

What the boy heard, and reluctantly revealed to Eli next
morning, was that God was about to exercise judgment on
the old man's household. The iniquity of his family could
not be expiated by sacrifices or offerings. Eli's guilt was that
he knew what others were doing and did not act to stop
them. It was indeed a sombre message for a young boy to
take to someone he admired, but Eli's response may have
softened the hurt: 'It is the Lord; let him do what seems right
to him' (3:18).

The story itself is, of course, crucial in the developing
saga of the birth of the Israelite monarchy. Samuel himself
would be appointed prophet of the Lord and, in response to
popular demand, he would anoint Saul, the disastrous first
king, and eventually David, his renowned successor.

Depth and honesty

Within the context of this book, however, I am interested in the picture of a relationship across the generations. Circumstances not of their choosing brought Eli and Samuel together, but there is a touching depth and honesty to their relationship. The frail and blind Eli depended on Samuel; the young boy drew strength, one assumes, from the elderly priest. The scene in which the terrible message is conveyed can be given many topical parallels: children find themselves in circumstances that require them to give support to a much older adult faced with personal or family tragedy, for instance.

Love knows no generational gaps. One of the weaknesses of modern life is that at times we seem intent on making those gaps unbridgeable. The church is as guilty, very often, as society at large. We segregate the congregation into toddlers, schoolchildren, youth, young families, older women and also men. We only have to look at a typical parish calendar to see what I mean.

I recall asking a teenager who had recently started coming to church with his friend what he made of it all. He thought for a moment. 'Well, it's OK. It's just a bit weird sitting in rows with people of all different ages.' So it wasn't the worship, the liturgy, the ritual (or even my sermons) that struck him as unusual, but the mixing up of the generations in the seating arrangements. It would never happen at school! Sadly, when it comes to activities beyond the morning service, the church, too, feels the need to divide us into our generational and gender groups—perhaps for excusable practical reasons, but at the expense of the richness of the whole.

The family was the ancient catalyst of love and respect across the generations, and in many cases it still is, but the catalyst requires contact. It's hard to build bridges across sensitive divides without frequent, almost daily, contact. For many people in our world today, that's not possible. Work, accommodation and finance issues may dictate that families live far apart and children only get to see Grandma and Grandpa once or twice a year. However, what the modern world takes away, it also restores: thank God for email, Skype and air travel!

Elisha and the young man

When an attendant of the man of God rose early in the morning and went out, an army with horses and chariots was all around the city. His servant said, 'Alas, master! What shall we do?' He replied, 'Do not be afraid, for there are more with us than there are with them.' Then Elisha prayed: 'O Lord, please open his eyes that he may see.' So the Lord opened the eyes of the servant, and he saw; the mountain was full of horses and chariots of fire all around Elisha.

2 KINGS 6:15–17

This is a classic old man/young man story. Elisha the prophet was getting old (we know that he was bald!) but he had a young servant who was with him when the place where they were staying was surrounded by enemy horses and chariots. Not surprisingly, the young servant was terrified. He turned at once to Elisha with dismay: 'What shall we do?'

The prophet spoke words of reassurance: 'Don't be afraid. There are more on our side than on theirs.' The servant could well have replied that it didn't look like it—an old man and his assistant on the one side and an army of horsemen and chariots on the other. Elisha's prayer changed the situation, however. He simply asked the Lord to open the young man's eyes so that he could see what Elisha knew but he didn't—that the hillside was full of horses and chariots of fire, presumably angelic, surrounding the prophet and his servant.

The incident highlights one of the few unquestionable advantages of age—experience. In Elisha's case we could add to that a tested and proven faith in God. Only those who have experienced the protecting hand of the Lord, who have found their prayers answered over the years, who know that, whatever the circumstances, they are never abandoned by the God they trust, could face this situation with equanimity. Elisha knew, from long experience, that they were not defenceless, but all he could do for the young man was to pray that his eyes would be opened to see the reality beyond reality.

The perspective of experience

It is one of the great gifts of age to see events through the perspective of a lifetime's experience. For the young, every event is a challenge or an opportunity that comes fresh from the twisting kaleidoscope of life. For the elderly, as the old Preacher says, 'there is nothing new under the sun' (Ecclesiastes 1:9). Sometimes we old men and women can be quite tiresome in our insistence that we've seen it all before, but very often it is a valid claim. Economic crises, wars and rumours of wars, unseasonal weather, corruption in high places—these have been the stuff of our daily lives over the decades.

In my own life I've lived through five or six major economic crises, each described in apocalyptic language by media commentators, each eventually resolving itself after a few years. I have also lived through several wars, some involving Britain, some simply causing general fear and stress about their wider consequences. I have never been one to say, 'Don't worry, it will all go away', but the fact is that even the worst of them have come to an end. It is one thing to sympathise with the victims, both of economic crises and of war; it is quite another to panic. Perhaps once again the role of the elderly is to persist in saying 'Keep calm and carry on'.

Wisdom without humility

The trouble with aged wisdom, as I remember from the days when I was the recipient of it rather than the dispenser, is that it can lack humility. We are not always right. Indeed, sometimes the message of the old is defeatist, while the temper of the young is positivity. The old say, 'Live with it; it's always been like that', but the young say 'I don't want to—I believe we can change the world.' It would be a sad day if the essential drive of youth to make things better were ever to be compromised by the essential caution of age. As in so many things, we need not one or the other but both.

In the story of Elisha and his servant, however, it is the young man who is defeatist and the old man who is positive—and Elisha's positivity is not born of arrogance but of faith, based on experience. If we who are old remember to speak primarily from faith and experience, we shall speak generously, as Elisha did, and be heard gratefully. We might also remember to our advantage that youth has its own messages and often they are full of hope and promise. Across the generations, we can support each other out of our present and past experiences. Elisha's prayer for eyes to be opened could also be a prayer for ears to be unstopped. We can be blessed by seeing and hearing wisdom, whatever its source.

Elizabeth and Mary

In those days Mary set out and went with haste to a Judean town in the hill country, where she entered the house of Zechariah and greeted Elizabeth. When Elizabeth heard Mary's greeting, the child leapt in her womb. And Elizabeth was filled with the Holy Spirit and exclaimed with a loud cry, 'Blessed are you among women, and blessed is the fruit of your womb. And why has this happened to me, that the mother of my Lord comes to me? For as soon as I heard the sound of your greeting, the child in my womb leapt for joy. And blessed is she who believed that there would be a fulfilment of what was spoken to her by the Lord.'

LUKE 1:39–45

From an old man and a young man we turn to an old woman and a young one—Elizabeth and Mary. This cameo, from the rich archives of the scriptures, has many of the distinctive traits of Luke's Gospel—human interest, powerful emotion, the beauty of relationships and the joy of simple things. It stands here immediately after the annunciation (the angel Gabriel telling Mary that she would be the mother of the Messiah) and immediately before Mary's great hymn of praise, the Magnificat.

Only Luke tells us in any detail of the events surrounding the birth of Jesus, and the only possible source of this information would have been Mary herself. Luke was writing about 70 years after the birth of Jesus, so she might well have been dead by then, but there is no reason why he could not have interviewed her beforehand: they both lived for a while in the same area of Asia Minor. According to tradition, Mary moved to Ephesus with the apostle John, who had been charged with caring for her by Jesus himself (John 19:26–27).

In any case, the story itself has all the hallmarks of authenticity. Elizabeth was shortly to be the mother of a son who would be known as John the Baptist. We've already mentioned the unusual circumstances of her pregnancy, seeing that she was 'getting on in years', as Luke puts it (1:7). She was, we have learnt, a kinswoman of the young woman Mary, who was betrothed to the carpenter Joseph and living in Nazareth in Galilee. Elizabeth lived about 60 miles away, we are told, 'in the hill country' of Judea to the south.

It would seem that very soon after the angelic visitation, the young Mary (by the betrothal customs of her time, probably still in her teens) decided to make that long journey to visit her elderly relative. This would hardly have been done on a whim. She had been told by the angel that her relative Elizabeth, in her old age, was now in the sixth month of pregnancy and the young girl must have been anxious to share her experience with someone else—someone she presumably knew and respected—who was also facing an unexpected and apparently miraculous childbirth. No mobile phones then, of course, or regular postal service, so we must assume that Mary simply turned up at the home of the elderly priest and his wife.

She entered the house and greeted Elizabeth, who told her that at the sound of her greeting 'the child leapt in her womb'. Pregnant women are used to that sensation, of course, so we must assume it was the precise timing that took Elizabeth by surprise. Her next words to Mary are familiar now as part of the 'Hail Mary' prayer: 'Blessed are you among women, and blessed is the fruit of your womb.' Her words doubtless reassured Mary, who had been 'perplexed' by the angel's greeting and was surely apprehensive about the astonishing role she had been chosen to fulfil—a role that many people, as the Gospels hint, were going to misinterpret (see John 8:41). Joseph had found it hard to accept and she knew that many people, even friends and relatives, might assume that the promised child was indeed the result of her misbehaviour.

The young woman reassured

To have her situation so comprehensively endorsed by the older woman, the wife of a temple priest and a respected senior member of her family, must have been enormously reassuring. Elizabeth called her 'the mother of my Lord' and affirmed that in believing the angel's promise and looking for its fulfilment, Mary would know God's blessing. No wonder Mary's response was a great outpouring of praise: 'My soul magnifies the Lord, and my spirit rejoices in God my Saviour' (Luke 1:46–47).

That is the biblical story told by Luke—a warm and human picture of two women, one very old, the other very young, finding in their encounter joy and reassurance. It can surely stand for thousands, perhaps millions, of similar human encounters in which women find strength and encouragement across the generational divide.

I remember a young woman in my church telling me that while she was at university she had got into difficulties. Because her parents had made such sacrifices to get her there and were so proud of her achievement, she simply didn't feel that she could talk to her mother about it. However, she had an elderly godmother with whom she was in regular contact, and she decided to phone and tell her about the mess she was in. The woman caught a train at once to the university town, met her, calmed her fears and went with her to speak with the college authorities. By the evening of that day, they had been able to go out for a meal together and really enjoy it.

Once again, the anxieties and fears of youth, fuelled by circumstances that had not been anticipated, were met by the confidence and experience of age. Within a few years, the young woman told me, their roles were somewhat reversed and she was able to offer her support to the older woman as she grew physically frail. They would meet up and read favourite poems to each other.

It seems that women are, by nature, better at 'networking' than men are—having a circle of friends with whom they can share joys, sorrows, disappointments and routine problems. When men meet, they tend to compete: 'I've got this new Honda, massive power, you should see it accelerate away from the lights.' When women meet, they tend to support each other. Usually this is within a generation band, but often the one person that a young woman will turn to in moments of genuine anxiety is an older woman.

A crucial moment

Many young expectant women, of course, turn to their own mothers for support and advice during their first pregnancy. After all, it is a new and daunting prospect—not only the nine months of physical and hormonal changes, but also the whole business of preparing for the birth and motherhood. When her mother is not around (and, in Mary's case, a mother is conspicuously absent from the biblical narrative) someone else, usually an older woman, relative or friend, steps into that role. Elizabeth was there at a crucial moment in the unfolding story of the birth and childhood of Jesus, and Luke's picture of this joyful encounter captures the beauty of the event perfectly.

Paul, Timothy and Mark

Let no one despise your youth, but set the believers an example in speech and conduct, in love, in faith, in purity... Do not speak harshly to an older man, but speak to him as to a father, to younger men as brothers, to older women as mothers, to younger women as sisters—with absolute purity.
1 TIMOTHY 4:12; 5:1–2

Get Mark and bring him with you, for he is useful in my ministry.
2 TIMOTHY 4:11

The relationship of the apostle Paul with his young lieutenants, Mark and Timothy, is a fascinating picture both of how things have changed and of how humans have always related to each other across the generational divide. Paul had met Mark, then probably aged about 20, possibly in Antioch, and recruited him as an assistant on his first missionary expedition with Barnabas, at some time towards the end of the fourth decade of the first century. This journey took them around the eastern Mediterranean, where they made many converts but also encountered some violent opposition, especially from militant Jewish groups. At one point Paul was stoned and had to be rescued by his companions. It may have been that this experience was rather overwhelming for the young Mark, who left the team in Pamphylia and made his way home.

When Paul and Barnabas planned a second similar expedition, they fell out over the inclusion of Mark in the team. Barnabas (his name means 'Son of encouragement') wanted to give the young man a second chance, but Paul was reluctant to take with them on a difficult enterprise someone who had 'deserted them in Pamphylia' (Acts 15:38). In the event, Mark ('John Mark' as Acts names him) went off with Barnabas, and Paul took Silas with him instead on his next expedition.

Timothy came on the scene probably 15 years or so later, when Paul was concerned with the supervision of the many churches he and his colleagues had planted in Asia Minor and Greece. He saw in Timothy, perhaps 30 years his junior, someone he could trust to share in that ministry. It would seem, from 2 Timothy 1:6, that Paul ordained him as a presbyter ('priest' in modern English): 'rekindle the gift of God that is within you through the laying on of my hands.' Both these young men, then—Mark and Timothy—at different times were working closely with an older and, in every sense, more senior person.

It's worth emphasising just how 'senior' Paul was. As an apostle, he was regarded in the early church with respect bordering on awe. After all, the apostles were the 'special messengers' of Jesus, witnesses of the resurrection (in Paul's case, not literally) and the foundation on which the Church was built. They were the men who, one of their critics said, were 'turning the world upside down' (Acts 17:6). Jesus had given them authority to 'bind and loose' sins, to be the repository of his teaching and to go into all the world and make disciples (Matthew 18:18; 28:19–20). You can't get much more 'senior' than that. Mark must have been deeply aware that it was an apostle, no less, whom he had abandoned in Pamphylia. Timothy must have recognised that these words of advice were much more than that: they were, to him, words of apostolic authority. The two young men, a generation apart, had both stood in the shadow of a spiritual giant.

'Get Mark'

Finally they are linked together. In his second letter to Timothy, written, it seems, while under house arrest and awaiting trial, Paul asks Timothy to 'get Mark and bring him with you'. Mark is a common name in the first century ('Marcus' in Latin, of course), so this might not be the same person as the young man who had deserted Paul in Asia Minor. However, a special 'Mark' clearly became an important disciple, the eventual author of the second Gospel, so it is quite likely that 20 years after that sad episode in Pamphylia, Paul had discovered that the young man he'd chosen to help him long before, who had caused him such disappointment then, was at last 'useful in my ministry'.

Probably Mark had changed—grown up and learnt that the path of discipleship is seldom easy. Possibly Paul had learnt, too, through testing years of travel, preaching and pastoral care, that it is foolish to discount someone on the grounds of one youthful error. Both, in other words, had learnt an important lesson. Paul now understood the enthusiasm, drive and fears of the young Mark. Mark probably now understood why, 20 years earlier, the apostle had doubted his commitment to the cause. It's only one small sentence, but it seems to encompass a lifetime of growth in wisdom, understanding and humility on the part of both men.

Paul's advice to Timothy not to let anyone 'despise his youth' is interesting. It may well be that he had done exactly that with Mark 20 years earlier, either not understanding what it was like to be a novice in an experienced team of older men or failing to appreciate how it felt for an inexperienced youth to face hostile and violent demonstrators. If it were true that Paul had been harsh in his assessment of Mark, clearly the passing years had amended his judgment. It was brave, surely, to appoint a young man like Timothy to a leading role in the government and pastoral care of the churches. After all, no one could become a rabbi until they had passed the age of 30 and the very title 'elder' speaks of a reverence for age and a reluctance to give leadership to younger people. Perhaps the memory of his experience with Mark had changed the apostle's view about the way he would treat younger people in the church.

What a lot can be read into that passing remark, 'Get Mark and bring him with you, for he is useful in my ministry'! Sometimes, those of us who are older are reluctant to admit to having made errors or misjudgments about people in the past. In fact, we are never too old to learn lessons.

Common-sense advice

The advice to Timothy has a great deal of common sense about it. Anyone who has been a teacher, minister or manager will recognise familiar potential pitfalls. Sometimes the danger is in being too assertive. I like 'do not speak harshly to an older man': I wonder if Timothy had done that and Paul had heard of it. Sometimes it's in being too familiar. There's a hint of that in Paul's caution about 'younger women'.

I did my National Service as a nursing assistant in the RAF. I worked on a busy ward in a hospital under a real martinet of a sister. She was reluctant to praise—I can't remember a single word of commendation, however hard we worked— and she was very conscious of her rank. After I had gone three weeks without a day off, I timidly approached her in her office to point this out. Her only response was to ask me if I was challenging her authority. Perish the thought!

On the other hand, on my next ward in the same hospital,

one of my colleagues became friendly with the rather attractive young sister (also, of course, a commissioned officer). They were both disciplined for 'over-familiarity': they had played tennis together on the hospital tennis court. I felt that somewhere between the two extremes, there might be a genuine way of working together across boundaries of seniority, age and rank.

Lessons learnt

Where Paul, Mark and Timothy are concerned, we get the impression that the apostle had learnt, over the years, some of the keys to working harmoniously and fruitfully with people of different ages. There is certainly a considerable difference of tone between the peremptory way Paul dealt with the failure of Mark on that first missionary journey—ignoring the views of his colleague, Barnabas—and his handling of potential problems in the case of Timothy. The young minister may have had difficulties with older men, senior women and young women; he may have been sensitive about his relative youthfulness; but the apostle's tone is constantly positive and encouraging.

Of course, in the context of this book, Paul (probably about 60 at the time) can hardly be classed as 'old'. He was, however, in the sort of position that many older people find themselves in, where their words carry influence, for good or ill, simply because of their seniority. This provides all the more reason to judge our words carefully, realising how damaging it could be to a novice Christian, for instance, to be rebuked or even gently ridiculed by a senior figure in the church. Old age can tend to produce a quite intolerant attitude, creating the impression that everything was so much better 40 or 50 years ago and that modern youngsters (by which we mean anyone under 60) are generally unreliable and frivolous.

In fact, old age and youth can live happily together, as most of us can testify. We don't get there by pretending that we are still in our teens (though 'cool', for instance, is such a lovely adjective) or by demanding that young people behave soberly and conservatively. If old age is to earn respect, it must be ready to give it, even to the youth club member who kicks a football against the car windscreen. After all, it's not unknown for us to break things, bump our cars into hitherto invisible bollards and forget to flush the loo. They put up with our funny ways; we learn to put up with theirs.

Jesus among the teachers

Now every year his parents went to Jerusalem for the festival of the Passover. And when he was twelve years old, they went up as usual for the festival. When the festival was ended and they started to return, the boy Jesus stayed behind in Jerusalem, but his parents did not know it. Assuming that he was in the group of travellers, they went a day's journey. Then they started to look for him among their relatives and friends. When they did not find him, they returned to Jerusalem to search for him. After three days they found him in the temple, sitting among the teachers, listening to them and asking them questions. And all who heard him were amazed at his understanding and his answers. When his parents saw him they were astonished; and his mother said to him, 'Child, why have you treated us like this? Look, your father and I have been searching for you in great anxiety.' He said to them, 'Why were you searching for me? Did you not know that I must be in my Father's house?' But they did not understand what he said to them.

LUKE 2:41-50

This is probably the ultimate 'young and old' story in the whole Bible, recounted with Luke's customary storytelling skill. Traditionally, Christian preachers have used it to demonstrate that, even aged twelve, Jesus knew his divine identity and was possessed of remarkable gifts of understanding. But the skilled pen of the Gospel writer also creates a human story with enormous empathy and insight.

Any parents of twelve-year old boys will recognise the scenario: their sons are confident enough to decide that they could look after themselves in the big city, ready with an answer for the inevitable anxious parental rebuke and oblivious to the pain and panic they might create by their actions. 'Why were you worried?' Only a twelve-year-old could say that to parents who, for three days, had feared they would never set eyes on him again.

That is the 'human interest' story, but behind it, of course, lies another one, which is the scene in the temple itself. There is an infamous (though brilliant) painting of that moment, *Jesus among the Doctors*, which is a forgery in the style of Vermeer by van Meegeren (1945). It shows a fair-faced boy debating with the astonished bearded teachers of the Law, asking them questions (which was normal) but apparently also offering answers (which was not). And those answers were not what they would have expected of a schoolboy: those who heard him were 'amazed at his understanding and his answers'.

We don't know what the rabbis made of this, but the clear impression is given that they too were impressed. At least, no one told Jesus to pipe down and leave the debate to his elders. They heard what he said, treated it seriously and engaged with him in an adult dialogue.

Engagement with the child

I feel there's a message here for those of us who are engaging with youngsters in Christian education. Perhaps the era of desperately patronising Sunday school 'lessons' is over—a story, a thought and probably a chorus to sing. David slew Goliath; the little boy brought his sandwiches to Jesus to feed the crowd; Zacchaeus climbed his tree to see the Saviour; there it is, offering no engagement with the children's own insights, ideas or questions.

Well, that era may be over, but often it is replaced with a slightly more sophisticated version of the same thing. The lesson goes ahead, there's a bit of handicraft or painting, a verse of the Bible is learnt, but the engagement between adult and child is minimal. The boy Jesus listened, asked questions and even dared to offer answers. Teachers are required to listen as well as talk—a truth that I took half a lifetime to learn and still often fail to recognise.

The interplay between Joseph, Mary and Jesus is also revealing. Luke says that the parents didn't understand what the boy said to them, but Jesus did not, at that moment, understand what they were saying to him either. 'Didn't you think how worried we would have been?' No, he didn't 'think', because twelve-year-old boys are not very good at reading adult responses to situations. For him, it all seemed crystal clear. He would be in the temple—'the Father's house', as Jews at the time called it. Why had they wasted time and trouble looking anywhere else? His answer, of course, completely failed to take into account how desperately worried they would have been at his initial absence from the village party on their homeward way.

Jesus, it seems, learnt quickly. He went back to Nazareth with his parents 'and was obedient to them'. Indeed, he 'increased in wisdom and in years, and in divine and human favour' (Luke 2:51–52). At the same time, no doubt, the young mother Mary and the older father Joseph had also learnt something about their young son, his nature and his destiny. No wonder Mary 'treasured these things in her heart' (v. 51).

The land of Long Ago

The relationship of parents to children is one thing, but in this book we are more interested in the relationship of children to grandparents and even great-grandparents. Happily, even those who do not have grandchildren usually have some children or young people in their circle of family and friends and the same principles apply.

I took the funeral of a 95-year-old man. Present at the service were about 20 youngsters, who spoke of his wonderful relationship with them. Some (teenagers, of course) were his grandchildren. Others, the youngest just two, were great-grandchildren. They all spoke of him as a wonderful friend, someone who talked to them as equals, was interested in what they did and told them stories of his own childhood. (At one time he was being brought up in the poorhouse, until his grandparents rescued him.) It was interesting to note their total disregard of his age as a factor in their relationship with him. I had seen photographs of family occasions, pictures that showed how easily he related to the youngsters, who seemed to congregate around his smiling presence.

The ability to connect

I don't suppose this man was particularly saintly (I don't know). What he had was humanity, and that translated into an ability to connect with people, especially young people. For some, that comes easily, as I suspect it did for him. For others, it's more difficult, though the difficulties are usually of our making, not theirs. We are inhibited by their youth, almost as if we feel like residents of an alien planet called Long Ago. We're afraid of looking ridiculous, of saying the wrong thing or putting our foot in it, but what they want is warmth, interest, confidence and friendliness. Age is surely no barrier to those. We can tell them about our lives, which to them are part of the history they learn at school. They can tell us about their lives, which are not as different from ours at their age as we might imagine. Across the decades, one human heart speaks to another. Sometimes it brings smiles and laughter, sometimes surprise, sometimes tears.

Yet the fact is that those of us who are old do often feel inhibited in our relationship with young people, even those we've known since they were born. From personal experience I have learnt, for instance, that it's unhelpful to ask the average teenager what school was like today. At best you'll get a grunt, at worst an awkward silence. Teasing a teenager about boyfriends or girlfriends creates embarrassment or, alternatively, silent resentment: you have ventured into private territory, something they only discuss with their closest contemporaries, who understand such things. So school and friends are probably best avoided.

That leaves, however, mountains of topics to explore, things in which we are *both* (and that's important) genuinely interested. They know, as we would, when someone is raising a subject not because they're genuinely interested in it but because it's a 'topic of conversation'. If we know them well, we shall be aware of the things they enjoy. It may be football, rugby, tennis, hockey. It might be contemporary music (difficult one that, unless you're a genuine aficionado yourself). It might be drama, fashion, Facebook or a favourite television programme. It might be places they've visited, perhaps on a school trip, which we also know. Put like that, their interests are not all that different from those of an 80-year-old.

The catalyst of humour

The best catalyst for any relationship, however, is humour. Those we can laugh with, we can live with. Sometimes children will laugh at us, which can take us aback but is actually a sign of acceptance. Yes, we can be odd because, let's face it, we're old. Old people do sometimes put on odd socks or get a famous name wrong or make little bodily eruptions that we hope others can't hear. Young ears will hear, but their laughter is not cruel, and joining in with it simply shows that we are part of the comedy, not an unwilling accessory to it.

Most children love their grandparents. It's a particular kind of love, born of familiarity and kinship but nourished by a 'lived in' relationship. We know them, possibly better than they know themselves, but they also know us, and that intimacy of knowledge binds us together in a sort of conspiracy of shared things.

One of those 'shared things' can be faith. Earlier in this chapter we considered Timothy's relationship with the apostle Paul, but even more formative in his life than the influence of the great apostle was that of his grandmother. She, we learn, was the original source of his faith. So we shall let the only grandmother identified as such in the New Testament (and possibly, depending on which translation you use, the whole Bible) stand tall in our last words on relationships 'across the generations'.

I am reminded of your sincere faith, a faith that lived first in your grandmother Lois and your mother Eunice and now, I am sure, lives in you.
2 TIMOTHY 1:5

8

Mood swings in old age

Do your best to come to me soon, for Demas, in love with this present world, has deserted me and gone to Thessalonica; Crescens has gone to Galatia, Titus to Dalmatia. Only Luke is with me... Alexander the coppersmith did me great harm; the Lord will pay him back for his deeds. You also must beware of him, for he strongly opposed our message. At my first defence no one came to my support, but all deserted me. May it not be counted against them! But the Lord stood by me and gave me strength.

2 TIMOTHY 4:9–11, 14–17

The writer is not a happy man. Deserted by friends, lonely, frustrated by opposition, confused by circumstances, he angrily denounces those who have let him down—though in pious terms, it must be admitted: 'May it not be counted against them'! All of this is ordinary enough, especially for someone who is clearly in a thoroughly unenviable position, possibly under house arrest and awaiting trial. But the 'someone' is the apostle Paul, the man who urges Christians not to be anxious, to fight the good fight of faith, to 'press on toward the goal' (Philippians 3:14). True, he is aware that in all of these troubles 'the Lord stood by me and gave me strength'. His real problem, it seems, is with his closest friends. Where were they when he needed them most? 'Only Luke is with me.'

Mind you, if I were alone, facing all these troubles and

perhaps feeling a bit depressed about them all, Luke would have been around the top of my list of desired companions. Luke was 'the beloved physician' (Colossians 4:14), who had travelled around Asia Minor with Paul, whom Paul had known for years—and a doctor! What more could you ask?

When we're feeling sorry for ourselves (and, with all due respect to the apostle, that's what this passage of scripture sounds like), even the presence of a friendly personal physician may not improve our mood. Most of us can identify with Paul's feelings entirely. We've been there and we know what it's like, and there's no doubt that feelings of this kind do tend particularly to overtake the elderly from time to time. We may be living on our own. We may not have seen other members of the family lately. Our best friend may be on holiday somewhere hot and far away. Then something happens and suddenly we feel incredibly isolated and alone. Where are they—and (we sometimes echo the psalmist) where is God, when we really need them?

I've called this chapter 'Mood swings in old age' not because younger people don't get them but because they can be a familiar feature of later years. When there were children around, work to go to, a partner always there when we needed them and friends always popping in, it would have seemed unthinkable that one day we would be living alone, waking in the night with a strange pain and wondering what it is, tripping the electricity and not being able to find a torch to locate the fuse box, suddenly anxious about tomorrow's arrangements or that odd noise coming from the boiler.

This second letter of Paul to Timothy is widely suspected by scholars of having been written largely by someone else. These intensely personal messages at the end, however, couldn't possibly have come from the hand of a secretary or one of his close associates after his death. These words are from the heart—painful, true to experience and about as close as we ever get to seeing the ordinary man Paul behind the public face of the apostle.

A cry for help

To be accurate, Paul wasn't really that old at this point, certainly not by modern standards (or Methuselah's). He was probably in his early 60s, but aware that life might well be moving into its closing phase, such was the opposition and downright hatred his work had evoked. Opinions vary as to when and where 2 Timothy was written, but in truth it doesn't much matter. Here is a man experiencing loneliness, abandonment, anxiety and opposition. His words are one of those 'cries for help' that counsellors talk about. 'I want you now, Timothy. And I want Mark. And my cloak (it's cold here of an evening) and the books. Until then I'll have to make do with Luke.'

The passage I quoted sits rather oddly with the rest of the letter, which is full of confident faith. These, for example, are the words that immediately precede it:

I have fought the good fight, I have finished the race, I have kept the faith. From now on there is reserved for me the crown of righteousness, which the Lord, the righteous judge, will give to me on that day, and not only to me but also to all who have longed for his appearing. (vv. 7–8)

Then comes the cry of the lonely heart, not bitter but bereft.

The dark cloud rises

Many Christians will have experienced precisely this paradox in their own lives. We have not lost our faith. We trust in the God who has accompanied us through the long years. Yet suddenly, from some inner wellspring of our hearts, the clouds rise and blot out the sun. Where is our loving God when we need him most? Where are friends, family, familiar things? Anyone who has read the Psalms will recognise the cry. They too are full of faith, praise and confidence, but then the same dark cloud appears:

Why, O Lord, do you stand far off? Why do you hide yourself in times of trouble? (Psalm 10:1)

How long, O Lord? Will you forget me for ever? How long will you hide your face from me? How long must I bear pain in my soul, and have sorrow in my heart all day long? (Psalm 13:1–2)

My God, my God, why have you forsaken me? Why are you so far from helping me, from the words of my groaning? (Psalm 22:1)

Be gracious to me, O Lord, for I am in distress; my eye wastes away from grief, my soul and body also... I am the scorn of all my adversaries, a horror to my neighbours, an object of dread to my acquaintances; those who see me in the street flee from me. (Psalm 31:9, 11)

My heart throbs, my strength fails me; as for the light of my eyes—it also has gone from me. My friends and companions stand aloof from my affliction, and my neighbours stand far off. (Psalm 38:10–11)

So cry several of the psalmists, and we can detect in their laments something of the feeling that Paul expressed in his dark moment of loneliness. More to the point, perhaps, there can be few people who have not felt exactly the same at some time in their lives. This is not anger or bitterness but simply the cry of bewilderment. We didn't think it was meant to be like this. Yesterday, all was well, so why do I now feel so isolated and helpless?

It would be wrong to imply that such feelings only come to the elderly. I can remember feeling rather like that at times as a teenager and several times during my adult life. There's no doubt, though, that because old people tend to spend more time on their own, and because many of our familiar loved ones, friends and even possession are no longer with us, the sudden realisation of our circumstances can bring clouds across the sunniest of evenings.

At the same time, it would be untrue to imply that old people spend days on end lamenting their plight. On the whole, my general impression and personal experience suggest that old age usually brings with it a degree of tranquillity. We don't have anything to prove any longer. We're not competing with anyone. Our ambitions are restricted to keeping the hedge trimmed or improving our basic skills at opening childproof medicine containers. We don't expect much— and 'blessed are those who expect nothing, for they shall not be disappointed'. Doctors will confirm that the elderly are neither in the high-risk category for suicide nor the prime consumers of tranquillisers. After all, we have the best one of all, a lunchtime nap.

Fears and regrets

Nevertheless, this generally placid scene is, for most of us, invaded by fears and regrets from time to time. They creep up on us unawares—and certainly uninvited. Sometimes an event, a person, a phone call or a letter may darken the hitherto cloudless sky. Sometimes we are hit by a sudden and acute awareness of isolation or a wave of regret for something precious that has been lost. It is then that we feel, as it seems the apostle Paul did, that we are on our own, struggling with our circumstances and with the desperate feeling that we can't cope with them. 'At my first defence no one came to my support, but all deserted me' (2 Timothy 4:16).

Loneliness

Loneliness is probably the most common trigger for a negative mood swing, as it seems to have been for the apostle. It's a strange feature of humanity that many of our 'boo' words are associated with it: alone, secluded, lost, friendless, abandoned, deserted, isolated, remote, solitary. Of course sometimes we enjoy our own company, but only if it's by choice: even a hermit has chosen to be one. The problem comes when the loneliness is not voluntary or becomes our daily pattern of life. There is something quite ominous about the phrase 'solitary confinement'.

It's possible to feel desperately lonely even in a crowd. I remember a young secretary at work telling me one morning that when she took her tube train ticket out of the machine, she said 'thank you' to it, because she hadn't spoken to anybody since she left work the previous evening—so it's not simply an old person's problem.

When it is, however, it somehow seems more serious or, at least, less easily corrected. My young colleague had plenty of friends and could have phoned one of them or made the effort to meet up somewhere. Very often, the old person has fewer social opportunities. Limited mobility, tiredness, not wanting to be a nuisance, dark evenings and the absence of those we could once have turned to at any moment: these are the barriers to familiar human contact.

Let me put it this way. When Paul was lonely he didn't want anyone, but someone: indeed, he named them. When an elderly person says that they're 'lonely', they don't usually mean there's no one around: they could try Tesco's, after all. They mean that those people—or often one particular person—who once provided companionship are there no longer. Of course it is possible to make new friends, but it's a fact that it gets harder as we grow older. There might be plenty of fish in the sea, but not all of them fancy the idea of spending time with a veteran member of the species.

Regrets, I've had a few

Regrets are another frequent trigger for sadness. The trouble with them is that they appear unannounced and when our defences are down. It's impossible to live to 80 and not regret some things that have happened in our lives—opportunities missed, friendships lost, errors and faults that, looking back, we recognise but can no longer rectify. There may be things we never did, apologies we never made, words of affection we never spoke. Anyone who says they have 'no regrets' has either got a short memory or very thick skin. Sorry, Edith Piaf!

I found an old letter that reminded me of how badly I'd

handled a very sensitive relationship long ago. Waves of regret swamped me. I felt very vulnerable, guilty, alone. I tapped my daughter's number into the phone and got voicemail. I rang the doorbell on my neighbour's house and got no answer. I shouted at God, but 'the heavens were like brass' (Deuteronomy 28:23).

That feeling passes, of course, thank God. Christian faith is about forgiveness and redemption, not the burden of unforgiven sin. Our default position is not despair but a form of hopeful contentment. Mood swings, however, are unexpected and exceptional. This is not how we see ourselves —it wasn't how Paul saw himself—yet in one sense the darkness is a valid part of our experience of life. Without it, we wouldn't know the meaning of the word 'light'. This is part of the reality of our human condition and it may well be that old age makes us slightly more susceptible to this expression of it. If so, perhaps that's not a cause for regret but for thankfulness.

Cultural alienation

Sometimes the dark clouds arise for the elderly through a feeling of alienation—not from people but from the contemporary society in which we find ourselves. It's hard to explain to younger people how revolutionary are the changes that have transformed almost every aspect of life and how daunting their impact can be on those who haven't grown up with them. It's not just technology (although that can be confusing enough) or the computer and the internet (even if we feel the whole world is now organised as though everyone except us is online all the time). Those of us born before World War II feel a bit like actors on a stage with the wrong scenery. What world is this? What language are they speaking, what principles do they live by and why is everyone talking at once?

Old people are sometimes accused of creating their own odd, exclusive clubs—Saga holidays, the Women's Institute, the Royal British Legion and so on. Wearily we try to explain: these are our familiar lands. They speak our language there. We can look at the Acropolis together or make jam or talk about National Service without having to explain what they mean to us or why we value them. It's not that we don't do 'modern'—we enjoy the benefits of science and technology as much as anyone else—but to us 'modern' is daytime television, the National Health Service, power steering and the deep-freeze, not Google, Twitter, Facebook and the inevitable invitation to 'go to our website'.

Of course, for many old people, including myself, the internet is an everyday boon and blessing. Grandparents can chat with their grandchildren in Australia by Skype, not only talking but actually seeing them. Those who live far from the big shops can order food, furniture and books online (and often get a welcome discount for doing so). Information is instantly available. The mobile phone has saved many elderly lives, at hand when we need it most—not like in the Welsh village of my childhood where the nearest telephone was two miles over the hills. We are not Luddites.

At the same time, we know that the landscape of life has changed drastically. It always does, of course, but I doubt whether things have ever before changed so swiftly and comprehensively. People themselves are much the same, but the things they do and their priorities in life have altered. My mother would ask her friends round for a nice cup of tea; my daughter meets her friends in Costa or Starbucks for a latte or an Americano. There's wi-fi on the buses and 'Anytime' on the television. The speed of one's broadband is a prime topic for male boasting. There is simply no escape from the incessant demand for communication. We are never free from emails and texts. With tablets and smartphones we can take the internet with us as our willing servant at the flick of a finger. We are stuffed full of information, but its sheer volume ensures that most of it is disregarded.

This may sound like a diatribe against progress, but in fact it is simply an attempt to explain to those who have grown up in, say, the last 25 years what today's society feels like to those of us who were in our 50s and 60s when the whole internet revolution began. We don't want it to stop. We just want younger people to understand our occasional difficulties with it.

Sometimes this feeling of being an alien in a strange land can be quite overwhelming. Imagine you are an octogenarian ringing a utility helpline. You are asked for passwords you've forgotten, customer numbers you never knew you had, overdraft facility figures you've never used—and all before you ever get to speak to a human being. No wonder, in sheer frustration and sometimes in tears, the older person simply gives up.

It's at that point that the cloud can begin to develop. This is not a familiar world and I feel a bit lost in it. Am I so useless that I can't cope with the circumstances I'm living in? And if I can't, what will become of me?

Failing powers

Probably the most insidious trigger for mood swings in the elderly, however, is the fear of steadily declining physical and mental health. It is a standard joke among my contemporaries that every time we can't remember a name or where we left the car keys or one of those wretched internet passwords, it is proof positive of the onset of dementia. As usual, we jest about what worries us and, as the years add up, it's completely natural to consider the seemingly inevitable consequences of ageing.

The trouble is that laughing about it doesn't always silence the interior voice pointing out that we do move more slowly now, do indeed sometimes forget things, occasionally trip over paving stones or carpets and find that the volume on the television mysteriously requires a few more decibels than it used to. Where, we wonder, will the process of decline lead? We think again of that gloomy portrait of geriatric failure in Ecclesiastes and imagine how it would affect our lives. Teeth, eyes, walking, thinking, remembering: what would life be like without them?

We are not so stupid as to think that we can miraculously be spared the inevitable slowing down of age or the various symptoms of a body and mind which, while serviceable enough at the moment, cannot be expected to go on for ever. Small events can trigger this particular cloud—a fall in the street, a silly mistake at the cash till, the embarrassment of forgetting the name of someone you see every week in church and have known for years. 'Is this it?' the anxious mind enquires, and the fear, once admitted, can speedily take over. In our imagination we are in a wheelchair or a residential nursing home or anxiously waiting for the home help to arrive to put us to bed.

This is not, we can note, a fear of the end but a fear of the last bit before the end. We see ourselves helpless, a nuisance or at least a burden, dependent on others in a way we have never been since we were weaned. It is not something we would choose for ourselves or wish on our nearest and dearest.

In my pastoral ministry I have spent a great deal of time with people who have actually arrived at that situation. The strange thing is that I can't remember any of them raging against their lot. Most of the time, they were simply grateful for the care they received, glad that family and friends were supportive and loving, and determined to live as fully as they could within the limitations of their circumstances. That is a tribute to the human spirit, which feeds on love and gratitude.

The mustard seed of faith

It is also very often a tribute to the value of faith in God, however minimal. After all, Jesus said that faith as tiny as a mustard seed could move mountains (Matthew 17:20). Those of us now in our 80s are members of a generation that had this kind of faith as a foundation on which everything else was built. Not every one of us is a practising, churchgoing, signed-up believer, but our generation was probably the last to have a kind of wired-in faith, born probably in Sunday school, tested and tried through wars and rumours of wars and all the knocks and blows of life. It's a generation that could say 'thank God' and actually mean it, said prayers at bedtime, enjoyed *Songs of Praise* on the television and was at home with the idea of living in a world created and loved by God.

It is so much easier for such a person to accept dependence —or, to put it another way, to accept loss of independence. Those who, in any sense of the words, see their lives as in the hands of God will find changes of this kind more acceptable.

'Into your hands, O Lord, I commend my spirit' is a simple but profound act of surrender. The words are simple but the message is profound.

Rescue from the mood swings

Not only in old age but at any age, we shall find it hard to avoid times when life seems to be lived under dark and cloudy skies. We have never been promised sunshine all the way. As I have just suggested, a simple faith in God is a fundamental antidote to despair, but it is not, as many of us can testify, a cast-iron guarantee that the clouds will never appear or return.

I know a woman of about my age whose faith had sustained her through many difficult episodes in life and who was regarded by all who knew her as an example of confidence in God. Yet recently she told me how she, too, had gone through a dark time of regrets and loneliness and even feeling abandoned. The medieval mystics called this experience 'the dark night of the soul' and for her it was both unexpected and unwelcome. A bereavement and moving home to an unfamiliar area had contributed, but the problem was essentially spiritual, as she recognised—and so, it proved, was the answer. She had not been abandoned by God. He was waiting, it seemed, for the right moment to lead her back into the light, so that she could share her experience with others and testify to the faithful love of God.

At the end of the passage from Paul's letter to Timothy with which this chapter began, there is a single sentence that seems to jump out of the page. For all his feelings of loneliness, of being abandoned by his friends, of isolation and anxiety, this is the apostle's last bold statement of faith:

'The Lord will rescue me from every evil attack and save me for his heavenly kingdom' (2 Timothy 4:18).

Interestingly, that's not a prayer. It is a simple, uncomplicated statement of faith. It recognises that 'attacks' will come but asserts that rescue from them is assured. I think that Paul's words very well encapsulate in religious language the ordinary everyday experience of many people. 'Attacks' may take different forms—circumstances, relationships, loneliness, anxiety—but so do the rescues. There is no formula or pattern to them. They come with many faces, perhaps through the intervention of a friend or the realisation that, despite appearances, we are loved and valued, not a 'burden' but a blessing. Rescue may come through an appreciation of the wonderful blessing of friends and family, of prayer and gratitude, of home and familiar things. For many of us, as for the apostle, it comes from the conviction that the God who has called us to faith and travelled with us through the ups and downs of life is unlikely to abandon us as we near the end of the journey. 'He will save me for his heavenly kingdom.'

9

Terminus or junction? Facing the last question

I had always assumed that when people passed 70, say, death became a major concern. After all, it was likely to be the next really important event in their lives. Surely old people would think about dying and death in much the same way as the teenager thinks of love and marriage, and the middle-aged of retirement, with a mixture of anticipation and apprehension? At least, I thought, they would talk about it a lot. When, at 59, I finally got to work full-time in a parish and to meet many older people living in that hinterland between fully active life and the gradual process of decline and inevitable death, I found I was both right and wrong.

I was right that they do talk about death—among themselves and with their families and friends, usually in a fairly light-hearted way. Phrases like 'when I pop off' and 'I won't be around then' are part of their everyday conversation. They plan for it, too, not just by writing a will but by thinking about the impact their death will have on their children and grandchildren. 'When I'm gone' is another popular phrase. It's not 'if' (because death doesn't give us that option) but 'when', and the event needs to be thought about and, as far as is possible, planned for. So, yes, they (we, now) do talk about death and dying.

On the other hand, I was wrong. I had assumed that old

people, living in the constant shadow of mortality, would have this looming terminus at the end of life's journey constantly in their thoughts. In fact, as I now know from personal experience, while old people often talk about death in terms of a future but as yet undated event, it is not a subject that dominates their thinking. Indeed, I doubt if the average elderly person thinks about death any more frequently than people 30 or 40 years younger. Partly, I suppose, that's because death is always something that happens to other people. Friends and relatives die and we go to their funerals, but (despite the best exhortations of the funeral service) that doesn't mean we go home and contemplate our own end. There are more pressing questions on our mind. What's for supper? Is *Lewis* on television tonight? Will the car pass its MOT?

In other words, like most people of any age, we live for the moment and certainly don't allow the looming figure of the Grim Reaper to cast a sickly pall over our daily lives. That doesn't mean, however, that we never think about what lies ahead or, from time to time, wonder what, if anything, lies beyond the unavoidable event of death. For most people, it's not an obsession. As a Christian minister, I could count on the fingers of two hands the number of people who have actually asked me to discuss with them the question of life beyond death, and several of those were people who were terminally ill.

Over 40 years ago I wrote a book, *Hereafter*, which set out the Christian 'case' for life after death. It was my only genuine bestseller, at a quarter of a million copies. Yet I cannot recall once being asked to speak at a meeting or church event on the subject, even though I'm used to being invited to speak about my books, even those that nobody seems to have bought. I can only suppose that people purchased it and read it (I know they did, because I've got a file full of letters) but were not keen to go public on their interest or discuss it with others. Death is not so much taboo as private.

Addressing the event

It seems to me ridiculous, nevertheless, to write a book about being old without addressing the most important single event that affects the lives of the elderly. 'It is appointed for mortals to die once, and after that the judgment,' writes the author of the letter to the Hebrews (9:27). It is inescapable and we know it, but it is also universal: it happens to everybody, and that somehow makes it easier. We aren't being picked on. We are in good company. Yet the fact remains: there is only one end to the journey of life and, for the elderly, it lies somewhere just ahead.

To think about what it means and, especially, whether death is (as I've tended to call it so far) a terminus or (as I would prefer) a junction, seems to be a rational part of the process of ageing. The great psychologist Karl Jung once said that no one can live in peace in a house that he knows is shortly to tumble about his ears. Contemplating death, then, is to face a resident but subconscious fear head on. It is not to be obsessive but realistic. Is there anything we can discover—any hints or images or insights—that will help us as we approach what we know is inevitable? Above all, is belief in life beyond death just whistling in the dark or are there reasonable grounds for it?

At this point, let's see what the New Testament has to say on the subject, as recorded by Paul in his first letter to the church at Corinth.

But someone will ask, 'How are the dead raised? With what kind of body do they come?' Fool! What you sow does not come to life unless it dies. And as for what you sow, you do not sow the body that is to be, but a bare seed, perhaps of wheat or of some other grain. But God gives it a body as he has chosen, and to each kind of seed its own body... So it is with the resurrection of the dead. What is sown is perishable, what is raised is imperishable. It is sown in dishonour, it is raised in glory. It is sown in weakness, it is raised in power. It is sown a physical body, it is raised a spiritual body... What I am saying, brothers and sisters, is this: flesh and blood cannot inherit the kingdom of God, nor does the perishable inherit the imperishable. Listen, I will tell you a mystery! We will not all die, but we will all be changed, in a moment, in the twinkling of an eye, at the last trumpet. For the trumpet will sound, and the dead will be raised imperishable, and we will be changed... Then the saying that is written will be fulfilled: 'Death has been swallowed up in victory.'

1 CORINTHIANS 15:35–38, 42–44, 50–52, 54B

Written in the debating style of the first century, this is not the easiest passage from the New Testament to understand, but one word clearly stands out: 'spiritual'. The point the apostle is trying to get across to the Corinthian Christians is that the resurrection—whether the resurrection of Jesus or of those who believe in him—is a spiritual event rather than a physical one.

This is quite difficult for human minds to comprehend. We are physical beings and we live in a physical universe. We are made of matter and deal with matter all day long. I suspect that's why most popular ideas of heaven, for instance, are really little more than a second innings of this life, but on a better wicket (to use a cricket analogy). So we make jokes about St Peter at the gates of heaven, letting some in (usually taxi drivers or curvaceous females) and keeping others out (usually vicars, mothers superior or even the Pope). We hear it all the time at funerals, in the family tributes: 'She'll be so pleased Andy Murray won a Grand Slam title at last' or, as I heard at a humanist memorial service, 'I like to think Neil's up there arguing with Mary about today's *Guardian* editorial'.

That's not what we actually believe, of course, but it's putting the mystery of death into a context we can at least understand. This very physical and 'earthy' impression of heaven—mansions, pearly gates 'up there'—may owe something to Victorian hymns, with their very literal representation of the allegorical and visionary language of the Bible, or to an obstinate but deep-rooted conviction on our part that death simply can't be the end and, if it's not the end, what can it be but more of the same?

Resurrection is an idea that is constantly misunderstood. It's not resuscitation. It's not our tired old bodies being re-conditioned and then placed in a new environment where they will never age or wither. It's not corpses leaving their graves, walking and talking (and reading the football results).

The only reliable model of resurrection, properly understood, is the resurrection of Jesus, and the passage we have read from 1 Corinthians 15 follows a trenchant defence and explanation of that resurrection. The Gospel accounts of it are not entirely consistent in their details, as though the writers were struggling to explain something that even they found inexplicable, but they are clear about one thing. Whatever the body was like in which the risen Jesus appeared to his friends, it was not 'physical', because physical bodies can't appear and disappear, pass through locked doors or travel quite long distances (Jerusalem to Galilee, for instance) without walking or riding.

I remember, when I was Head of Religious Broadcasting at the BBC, being quizzed by the head of the Gallup polling organisation over the response given by Church of England bishops to what he thought was a straightforward question put to them by his researchers. It came after some public pronouncement, possibly by the then Bishop of Durham, which appeared to question the literal truth of the resurrection of Jesus. The question posed, to which a straight 'yes' or 'no' answer was required, was this: 'Do you believe in the physical resurrection of Jesus?' He couldn't understand why not one bishop would answer the question. They all wanted to quibble about the word 'physical'. They believed in the resurrection of Jesus but couldn't square that particular adjective with the biblical records. Indeed, in 1 Corinthians 15, Paul says categorically that 'flesh and blood cannot inherit the kingdom of God' (v. 50).

The New Testament tells us three things that God 'is': God is love (1 John 4:16), God is light (1 John 1:5) and God is spirit (John 4:24). We may talk of God's hands or eyes or face, but the old Thirty-nine Articles of the Church of England surely get it right when they say that God is 'without body, parts, or passions'. When we say that God is 'spirit', we are acknowledging that he is fundamentally different from us. He is not matter. He is not defined by the physical world or restricted by it, as we are, and the world of the resurrection is 'the kingdom of God', not planet earth or any other location in the universe.

This seems to me to be the truth that Paul is labouring as he explains, for the benefit of the Christians at Corinth (and, down the centuries, for us), what 'resurrection' means. To be resurrected is to move from one dimension of existence, the physical, into another dimension of existence, the spiritual. For him, that is not loss but gain—the spiritual body is glorious, he says, and powerful and honourable, while the physical body is 'perishable', like an item of food beyond its 'use by' date. Our bodies are created to live in the physical world. To enter the 'kingdom of heaven' we shall need a new vehicle for our personalities, a 'spiritual' body.

That does not mean we move from being a 'person' to becoming a ghost. We can imagine the apostle's horror at that suggestion! Nor is it a 'second best', a shadowy existence without form or personality. It is in every way superior to the life we have lived on earth. The resurrected body is better in every respect, not just because it doesn't age or wear out but because it is in its perfect environment. It was never our destiny as human beings to end up as a handful of dust on the surface of a dying planet, but to be alive with all the life of God in the mysterious but glorious world of the spirit. So Paul ends his explanation in triumphal style. The 'trumpet will sound and the dead will be raised'. Those of us who are still alive on earth when this happens 'will all be changed... in the twinkling of an eye' and death will be 'swallowed up in victory'. The language is visionary rather than literal, but the message is plain. The physical comes first, but then, when it dies (like a seed in the ground), it is reborn as spiritual. That, Paul says, is resurrection.

What about heaven?

Resurrection, you may say, is at least comprehensible, but that leaves the whole question of heaven. I have already mentioned the stubborn and deep-rooted persistence in human beings of an instinctive belief in an 'afterlife'. That afterlife has form, personality and, often, a place in which to express itself. Throughout recorded human history, people in most cultures have had such a belief—Valhalla, the Elysian Fields, reincarnation and Nirvana, the abode of the dead in ancient Egypt, Abraham's bosom and the Christian heaven.

In modern society, however, the idea of 'heaven' has become a considerable stumbling block to faith. While we often use the language of the hereafter (as we have seen), the whole idea of heaven as a 'place' where life continues for ever stretches our credulity. Old people, every bit as much as young ones, ask the same questions. What, where and how is 'heaven'? How are we to interpret it in the light of our present-day understanding of the universe? Indeed, is it possible in the 21st century to believe in the biblical picture of the kingdom of God, the 'new Jerusalem'?

The splendid but gloriously metaphorical last chapters of the book of Revelation have been the source of much Christian art, hymnody and devotion.

And in the spirit he carried me away to a great, high mountain and showed me the holy city Jerusalem coming down out of heaven from God. It has the glory of God and a radiance like a very rare jewel, like jasper, clear as crystal. It has a great, high wall with twelve gates, and at the gates twelve angels, and on the gates are inscribed the names of the twelve tribes of the Israelites... And the wall of the city has twelve foundations, and on them are the twelve names of the twelve apostles of the Lamb... The wall is built of jasper, while the city is pure gold, clear as glass. The foundations of the wall of the city are adorned with every jewel... And the twelve gates are twelve pearls, each of the gates is a single pearl, and the street of the city is pure gold, transparent as glass. I saw no temple in the city, for its temple is the Lord God the Almighty and the Lamb. And the city has no need of sun or moon to shine on it, for the glory of God is its light, and its lamp is the Lamb. The nations will walk by its light, and the kings of the earth will bring their glory into it. Its gates will never be shut by day—and there will be no night there. People will bring into it the glory and the honour of the nations. But nothing unclean will enter it, nor anyone who practices abomination or falsehood, but only those who are written in the Lamb's book of life.

REVELATION 21:10–12, 14, 18–27 (ABRIDGED)

For the most part, people today don't relate to gates of pearl and streets paved with gold. We can't imagine a massive piece of real estate, large enough to accommodate the millions and millions of people who are to be its joyful residents, floating around somewhere in the universe. The imagery of Revelation, so persuasive and attractive to past generations, strikes us as bizarre to the point of incredibility.

Our hymns don't help. 'Prostrate before thy throne to lie / And gaze and gaze on thee': really, for all eternity? The gazing will, it appears, be accompanied by the endless sound of harping and worship that also never ends. Is our eternal destiny really to be so utterly passive? No wonder many present-day people, including many devout Christians, are a bit dubious about the attractiveness of 'heaven' as it is usually portrayed—and as these last chapters of the Bible, taken literally, seem to picture it.

Of course we can't 'imagine' heaven because it can't possibly be anything like our present existence. As we have seen, it is not part of the physical, material world with which we are familiar. Confusingly, for us, it is also outside time, so to call it 'everlasting' life is to give entirely the wrong impression. It is 'eternal' in the way that God is eternal— simply 'existing', the 'I am' of the burning bush (Exodus 3:14), the permanent present tense. Heaven requires us to think spiritually, beyond our familiar environment of time, space and matter. The whole idea stretches our earthbound imaginations to breaking point.

But then, the baby in the womb could not possibly 'imagine' what our familiar human life involves—walking, making love, driving cars, gardening. The baby is, we're told, reluctant to be squeezed out of the comfort of the womb into the unknown and frightening world outside, all lights and noise and strangeness. No wonder the first thing a baby does is cry!

Once we are into human life, though, which of us would opt to go back into the womb for ever? Perhaps we shall feel the same after death—an event we dreaded or, at any rate, feared because of its unknown nature. Like the baby, we're reluctant to move from a familiar zone into an utterly new one, but perhaps, having moved, we would be even more reluctant to come back.

Jesus often spoke about 'the kingdom of heaven' but almost entirely in comparisons—'the kingdom of heaven is like…' followed by pictures of a field with both corn and weeds in it, a net enclosing a vast catch, a tree growing from a tiny seed, treasure hidden in a field and a pearl of great value. All of these images speak of life and growth, of beauty and value, of challenge and opportunity. That, said Jesus, is what the kingdom of heaven is 'like'.

He said nothing about how extensive it is or where it is located or what it looks like, but he made it clear that God his Father is there: indeed, heaven is where he is and where his perfect will is done. It is God's 'kingdom'. He also said that it has many 'dwelling-places' (John 14:2) and that he would prepare some of them for his disciples. This is not the language of literal facts, of course. I don't think I will be booked into number 39 Pearly Gates Way on an eternal lease. However, Jesus is asserting that heaven is real, a 'place' (though not a spot in cosmic geography), and offers a 'home' of permanence and love.

A perfect place

As Revelation makes clear, heaven involves the total abolition of all that is evil. This is life without anger, hatred, lying, suffering, pain or death. And that's it, really. All the beautiful pictures of golden streets, harvests twelve times a year, jewel-encrusted gates and trees with healing leaves are there to tell us that this is a perfect place to be. The city's gates are not locked because there are no thieves and everyone is welcome. Heaven is all we could wish for, all that human life struggles and longs to be. This is a place of fulfilment, growth, discovery and endless activity: 'his servants shall serve him' (Revelation 22:3, KJV). So much for 'resting in peace'! It is a place where we shall be more alive than we have ever been, more loving and more loved. It is, in a memorable phrase of the apostle Paul, the place where 'together… we will be with the Lord for ever' (1 Thessalonians 4:17)—and 'together' means with those who have died before us (v. 13).

Jesus told his disciples, just before his own death, that he was going to 'prepare a place' for them, 'so that where I am, there you may be also' (John 14:3). Heaven, in other words, is where he is, and where he is is with the Father. That is probably all we need to know about heaven: indeed, that is just about all we do know for certain about it. For those of us on the threshold of eternity, that relationship with our Creator and our Saviour is, more than anything else, the ground of our hope.

Belief in the 'hereafter'

The percentage of people in the UK who believe that there is life beyond death has tended to decline over recent years. Oddly, in some ways, that decline has been more evident among older people than younger ones: a BBC opinion survey in 1995 was the first to detect it. Many of my contemporaries hold to the 'out like a light' theory of death. A few prefer to think of some kind of reincarnation—the soul returning to an earthly body. The number holding to the full and particular Christian doctrine of the resurrection (as set out above) is manifestly shrinking, though almost half the population say that they believe it.

I don't find any of this surprising. Belief in life after death requires a big intellectual leap. It is interesting that in AD54, a mere 20 years after the first Easter Day, there were people in the church at Corinth who were struggling to believe it. It is obviously something that, by its very nature, can be neither proved nor disproved.

I think that many who do hold the Christian position on eternal life do so for two reasons—which I share. The first is that, beyond doubt, Jesus believed it. However you read the Gospels, that can't be denied. So, if the Son of God believed it and argued the case with passion and eloquence, who am I to disagree? In other words, belief in a resurrection flows from a belief in Jesus.

The second reason is what I shall call personal experience.

I don't, of course, mean experience of living on the other side of death, but events, powerful impressions, even significant signs that have accompanied the death of someone close to me. I watched my wife die in hospital and, within two or three days, knew (and I choose the verb carefully) that she had not ceased to exist. The experiences were too intimate and private to put into print, but I have found that many other people in my position have had similar and equally convincing evidences that personal life, in a spiritual sense, does not terminate when this earthly body breathes its last. I realise that this is not 'evidence' for anyone else, but the cumulative experience of so many people down the centuries must offer some kind of support for the arguable but unprovable case set out by Paul, which has been the teaching of the Christian Church throughout its history.

Does belief help?

Does this kind of belief make a decisive difference to the well-being and happiness of the old person? That's not as easy to answer as it might sound. I know people without any religious faith who seem to approach death with equanimity, just as I have ministered to people of faith who have found the whole prospect distressing.

In general, however, my experience is that those with a strong belief in life beyond death, based on a considered and serious faith commitment, face the onset of death with a high degree of calm. Of course, the unseen and unknown is always unsettling. Few Christians could equal the confidence of a friend of mine who sent a text message from hospital just a few hours before she died, observing that 'death is so exciting'. At the same time, I have never seen terror in the eyes of a dying person, believer or not, and often a sudden surge of faith towards the end brings a quiet acceptance that their time has come.

Dylan Thomas, in a striking poem, urged his dying father to 'go not gentle into that good night', but to 'rage against the dying of the light' (1951). I think that is very much a younger person's view of the way in which an old person might see the approaching end. We who are old are not much given to 'raging' about such things. We reserve real rage for keys we can't find, cooking instructions in tiny print and endless repeats on summer television. Why waste good anger on something you can't possibly change or avoid?

The night prayers, Compline, include a repeated petition: 'Into your hands, O Lord, I commend my spirit'. Whether we actually say the words or not, I think a lot of us go to bed at night in that attitude. We expect to wake up the next morning but accept that one night we might not. There isn't much we can do about it except to place ourselves into the hands of the One who first gave us life and who, in the ultimate sense, determines when that earthly life shall end. Rage is altogether too violent and negative a reaction. Head on the pillow, reflections on the day that is past, and then 'Into your hands, O Lord': what more could one ask?

10

At the end of the day

It is my eager expectation and hope that I will not be put to shame in any way, but that by my speaking with all boldness, Christ will be exalted now as always in my body, whether by life or by death. For to me, living is Christ and dying is gain. If I am to live in the flesh, that means fruitful labour for me; and I do not know which I prefer. I am hard pressed between the two: my desire is to depart and be with Christ, for that is far better; but to remain in the flesh is more necessary for you.

PHILIPPIANS 1:20–24

To pick up again the railway metaphor—terminus or junction —this final chapter is about living life right up to the buffers. I've chosen this passage from Paul's letter to the church at Philippi as an example of someone wrestling with this very challenge. There is a good deal of scholarly dispute about the provenance of this letter, but what seems certain from internal evidence is that, at the time of writing, Paul was under some kind of arrest and recognised that his life was in danger. He had a particular affection for the Philippians and here he shares with them the tension in his own mind. The phrase 'by life or by death' shows his thinking, and it leads into a fascinating disclosure of a personal dilemma.

Supposing he were to be put to death? Well, he says in effect, that's fine. I would 'be with Christ' and that is 'far better'. 'Far better' than what? Imprisonment or a resumption of his normal life? He doesn't say, but 'far better' is clear enough in one sense. To die would mean being 'with Christ' and it is that situation which is, for him, 'far better'.

On the other hand, he argues with himself, to remain alive in the flesh would mean he could continue his present 'fruitful labour'. This 'fruitful labour' is not for his own benefit, he claims, but for the Philippians, though it is obvious that Paul himself derived great fulfilment from his work. Would he prefer to 'go' (and be with Christ) or remain, presumably free once again to travel and continue this fruitful ministry? He is very honest about the dilemma: 'I do not know which I prefer.'

The good news, for Paul and for all of us, was that he would not have to make the decision himself. A tribunal in Rome might release him, which would presumably mean 'fruitful labour' again, or the sword might fall and he would be 'with Christ'. The decision would not be his. He might eventually have worked out a preference but, unless he contemplated suicide, the decision was out of his hands. He would undoubtedly have seen that decision as lying ultimately not with any human court but with God himself. His life was in God's hands, not Caesar's.

There may come a time in life when each of us wonders whether it is any longer 'worth living': I'm thinking of extreme physical or mental disability or infirmity, or even a profound feeling of uselessness. We may not know which we 'prefer', life as it is or death and whatever lies beyond it—but, as it was for the apostle, the choice is happily out of our hands. 'The day thou gavest', as the hymn says, is also the day that draws to a close, but we determine neither the date of our birth nor, under normal circumstances, the date of our death. It is not for us, any more than it was for Paul, a matter of our 'preference'.

What is interesting in his analysis of the dilemma is that he doesn't mention a third option—buying a pair of slippers, finding an easy chair and simply retiring from the business of daily living. He accepts that he might be put to death, but the alternative for him is not simply to go on existing but to go on living as fully as possible. 'Fruitful labour' suggests fulfilment, not futility.

Fulfilment in old age

Different old people find fulfilment in different ways. For many, the primary source of it is the family—children, grand-children and great-grandchildren. Their role becomes as a genial, much-loved symbol of the family's unity. They enjoy the company of the younger generations, take an interest in what they do—their achievements and their setbacks—and are invariably included in family occasions. Their homes are adorned with multiple framed photographs: 'That's Annabel,' you'll be told. 'She's just got engaged to such a nice young man. Oh, and that's Henry—he's at university. Always was a bright lad.' So they can take you through the family archives, as it were, each member being equally noted and equally valued.

This is, I suppose, the traditional role of the elders in a family setting, and there's no doubt that it can be a very ful-filling one. We feel an essential part of a living community and, no matter what happens to us in terms of physical or mental decline, we know that we shall be, to the end of our days (and beyond), 'Grandpa' or 'Grandma'.

Not everyone, by the nature of things, can enjoy such a family role, of course. There are those who were never married and have no children (and hence no grandchildren), although often they will have nephews and nieces or godchildren who fulfil much the same role. There are those who have had a marriage breakdown or have suffered the pain of family division. There are those who, for reasons of circumstances or geography, are far removed from the rest of their family. Sadly, there are situations in which the younger family members don't wish to accord to elderly relatives that kind of patriarchal or matriarchal role. The fault may lie with either party or simply with different ways of seeing family relationships. It can, however, be very painful for the older person and a genuine loss of something valuable for the younger ones.

The family is by no means the sole source of potential fulfilment for the elderly. A much-loved cat or dog can serve as a companion and also as a welcome responsibility. Friends are increasingly important and valued as we get older (and as death reduces their numbers). One of the recurring problems, however, is that of keeping in touch when separated from friends by distance. I think this is why so many old people have taken avidly to email. We can keep in touch and even have a stored record of our contacts with friends at a fraction of the cost of letters or phone calls. The addition of Skype, of course—with the chance to see each other as well as to read words—makes electronic communication only a hug short of perfection.

Radio and television

Radio and television are also important in the lives of the elderly. Instead of feeling a bit guilty about 'wasting time watching the box', we can argue that years of abstinence have now justified the indulgence. I admit that my radio comes on at 7 o'clock every morning and that, if I am home in the evening, the television is my constant source of mental stimulus and pleasure—as well as occasionally reducing me, in the manner of the old, to impotent fury. As it becomes more difficult to get out to events—meetings, concerts, even services—especially in bad weather, the radio and the television provide immediate voices and images. Having worked in both for many years, I sometimes feel that those in charge of broadcasting nowadays forget what a huge, loyal and enthusiastic potential audience there is among the over-80s. We don't want geriatric broadcasting but we do appreciate quality, style, warmth and familiarity.

Books and magazines

While eyesight remains adequate, reading is another great source of fulfilment for the elderly. The library is an Aladdin's cave for the older reader, a treasure house of delights. I have a sister-in-law who reads endlessly about history, buildings, monuments and old churches. Indeed, she has made herself into an expert on the subjects. Others—and not only men— enjoy reading about sport, especially cricket, which has a rich heritage of literature. Many women prefer fiction. It can't be coincidence that P.D. James is still writing bestselling crime novels in her 90s!

Many in old age turn with fresh enthusiasm to the Bible. I know that's true because I meet them at 'teaching days' and retreats. I find that it is often older people who are most keen to tackle what are regarded as the most 'difficult' books— Ezekiel, Leviticus, Romans or Revelation. Perhaps struggling with teasing and profound ideas appeals to those who at last have time to wrestle with the mysteries of eternity, purpose and life itself. I know from experience that older people often ask the most searching questions—not the 'how?' of younger years but the 'why?' of the questioning heart.

Faith and religion

It is an observable fact that many old people find great solace in their religious faith. Church congregations are, on the whole, made up of the Saga generation. One cynical observer accused them of 'swotting for finals'—one last effort, as it were, to make it through those pearly gates. As I have already suggested, however, it simply is not true that old people, in or out of church, are obsessed with death, heaven, hell and the Last Day. I don't think many go to church to earn Brownie points for the final judgment!

Still, for whatever reason (and my hunch is that it's largely the result of having more time to think and fewer daily distractions), faith is important for many old people. I don't find this depressing or a reason for the churches to panic. They do sometimes seem guilt-stricken by the fact that teenagers, young adults and even middle-aged men do not, generally speaking, figure very largely in regular Sunday congregations. Much the same is true, after all, about Radio 4. I can remember hand-wringing conferences at the BBC about the channel's failure to attract young listeners, but if they turn up in the end—if there is a natural progression that almost inevitably leads the teenage devotee of Radio 1 to end up with Radio 4 in their 60s—what's the problem? 'Turning up in the end' does sometimes seem the fashion in church. Of course, Christians would like to see more young families and children learning the value of faith and worship. Yet surely, whether it is early or late, 'anyone who wishes' may come and drink the water of life (Revelation 22:17). There is no age qualification for salvation.

In fact, pastoral experience confirms that many old people find, or rediscover, a living faith. As I've suggested, this is less a matter of preparing for the end than making a fresh beginning, often prompted by having the time to think things through. Life from teens to retirement is often one long rush, a hectic trip from somewhere to somewhere (or occasionally nowhere to nowhere). Family, money, work, holidays, hobbies: there never seems to be quite enough time to stop and think. One of the real blessings of age is space and time, and out of it often comes a new appreciation of what is really valuable and eternal. As the psalmist says, 'Be still, and know that I am God' (Psalm 46:10).

At the (very) end of the day

When David's time to die drew near, he charged his son Solomon, saying: 'I am about to go the way of all the earth. Be strong, be courageous, and keep the charge of the Lord your God, walking in his ways and keeping his statutes, his commandments, his ordinances, and his testimonies, as it is written in the law of Moses, so that you may prosper in all that you do and wherever you turn.'
1 KINGS 2:1–3

The opening chapters of 1 Kings are a fascinating account of the last days of Israel's greatest king, David. He had become very frail: indeed, he was at one point so cold that his advisors enlisted a buxom young woman to get into bed with him to warm him up (1:1–4). It seems to have worked, although I suspect it would be pointless asking the NHS for that particular treatment nowadays.

For the most part, these chapters describe a procedure that often gives old people a strange sense of satisfaction and fulfilment—winding up their affairs, dealing with unfinished business, ensuring that 'at the end of the day' they will have few regrets about unresolved issues or problems left for their executors to deal with. For David, these issues included, in the manner of the time, a few old scores to be settled (2:5–6), a few kindnesses to be repaid (v. 7) and a very generous provision for the grandson of his one-time would-be assassin, King Saul (2 Samuel 9:1–7). He also, as one does, felt free to dispense some sage advice to his own son, Solomon (1 Kings 2:1–4).

I am no King David: I have no old scores to settle and certainly no throne to pass on to my eldest. However, I have been surprised to find how rewarding it is to write a will. This may be because it looks beyond the end of our own earthly life and concerns the lives of those we cherish and the support of causes that we have valued during our lives. It has a whiff of continuity about it. More than that, however, it is an act of finality, a kind of drawing together of the events and preoccupations of our lives and passing them on to our successors. It has slightly the same feeling as settling an argument before bedtime ('Do not let the sun go down on your anger', Ephesians 4:26) or paying a bill that has been in our in-tray for too long.

Of course, we usually do not know when the very end of the day will come. This seems to me all the more reason to ensure that, when it does, we are not found to have left a legacy of muddle or confusion for those who pick up the pieces. Not only that: as I have said, there is a strange sense of fulfilment in doing it. King David—who, after all, had not led an entirely blameless life—sets us an example. We can't, in our humanity, be perfect, but we can be tidy!

And after that? All of this brings us to the small matter of 'shuffling off this mortal coil', as Shakespeare so elegantly put it. David, in 1 Kings 2, also has a nice turn of phrase:

'I am about to go the way of all the earth'. The actual event is recorded in traditional terms: 'Then David slept with his ancestors, and was buried in the city of David' (v. 10).

Sooner or later, this is indeed 'the way of all the earth'. There are many euphemisms for it—'falling asleep', 'passing away', even (in Salvation Army language) 'being promoted to glory'—but they all describe the same terminal event, the end of a mortal life. Not surprisingly, those of us who are old do sometimes wonder what the reality will be like.

I worked at the BBC for several years with the poet John Betjeman. Those familiar with his work will know that his poems often expressed something approaching terror about the actual business of dying—in which cottage hospital would it occur, would the sheets be wet with the dying man's sweat, and so on. We talked about it a few times and I have a letter from him, written not long before his death, expressing a newfound degree of confidence about the event. It was consequently reassuring to hear that he was translated to the next world while fast asleep in a deckchair in the garden of his beloved Cornish home.

Not all deaths are that easy, of course, but modern palliative medicine ensures that most of them are relatively pain-free and peaceful. I had a near-death experience some years ago in the Accident and Emergency unit of the Bristol Royal Infirmary. I gather that the nurses and doctors were extremely busy on my behalf and the friends who had brought me in were very anxious, but I simply lay there, conscious but in a state of almost blissful detachment. After I recovered, I took from it a new awareness that things are often different inside from how they appear outside.

There is a very precious time for me every day, somewhere between the end of deep sleep and the onset of true waking, when I seem to be in a kind of transitional existence. During that period, which on a good day might be an hour and a half, I may daydream, half awake, or even perhaps be in a state of enhanced spiritual awareness. Lying there, the unshackled mind knows no bounds. All the events of my life are available, as if a giant archive has been opened and its pictures presented before me. People, places, ideas, phrases of poetry, lines of hymns, scenes from childhood and moments of joy, regret, gratitude and sorrow are momentarily relived. Then, just beside my head, comes a voice: 'It's seven o'clock on Tuesday the ninth of October. Here are the news headlines.' Radio 4 has summoned me back into the present. I was going to say 'reality', but which is actually more real?

The writer and broadcaster Malcolm Muggeridge, a major media figure in my lifetime, came to Christian faith late in life. He wrote this when he first became aware of the onset of old age.

> As the old do, I often wake up in the night and feel myself in some curious way, half in and half out of my body, so that I seem to be hovering between the battered old carcass that I can see between the sheets and seeing in the darkness and the distance a glow in the sky, the lights of Augustine's City of God. In that condition, when it seems a toss up whether I return to my body to live out another day, or make off, there are two particular conclusions, two extraordinarily sharp impressions that come to me. The first is that of the incredible beauty of our earth—its colours and shapes, its smells and its features, of the enchantment of human love and companionship, and of the blessed fulfilment provided by human work and human procreation. And the second, a certainty surpassing all words and thoughts, that as an

infinitesimal particle of God's creation, I am a participant in his purposes, which are loving and not malign, creative and not destructive, orderly and not chaotic, universal and not particular. And in that certainty, a great peace and a great joy.

QUOTED IN RICHARD INGRAMS, *MUGGERIDGE: THE BIOGRAPHY* (HARPERCOLLINS, 1995)

'Your old men shall dream dreams,' quoted the apostle Peter on the day of Pentecost (Acts 2:17). Malcolm Muggeridge's dreams (or are they visions?) came in the night watches. Mine come in the early hours. I don't think of them, and nor did he, as the confusions of age, but as the clarity of vision that comes with the dawning of a new day.